GW01315781

NORFOLK COUNTY LIBRARY
WITHDRAWN FOR SALE

MY TRAVELS WITH WHEELY

Nicky Dalladay

authorHOUSE®

AuthorHouse™ UK Ltd.
500 Avebury Boulevard
Central Milton Keynes, MK9 2BE
www.authorhouse.co.uk
Phone: 08001974150

© 2011 Nicky Dalladay. All rights reserved.

No part of this book may be reproduced, stored in
a retrieval system, or transmitted by any means
without the written permission of the author.

First published by AuthorHouse 2 January 2011

ISBN: 978-1-4520-6487-1 (sc)

This book is printed on acid-free paper.

ACKNOWLEDGEMENTS

My gratitude goes to:

Simon Child, for designing a fun cover encapsulating my outlook.

Wendy Russell, Madeleine Hatwell, and Cheryl Schofield who read and commented on the manuscript, and continually encouraged me.

Richard Day and Natasha Harri, for designing a guide to our journey, and with their skills removed the odd, unwanted tourists from the pictures.

Our friends' continued support mentally, emotionally, and physically.

ABOUT THE AUTHOR

Nicky Dalladay used to be a resident of the able-bodied world, living a normal life, enjoying just about everything. Suffice it to say, life was fun. She spent her career discovering who she was by trying a variety of different jobs, finally ending up where she wanted to be. At a young age she was diagnosed with secondary progressive multiple sclerosis but, she decided to put this condition on a back burner. There just weren't enough hours in the day to waste time thinking about illnesses. Having a sense of fun was always most important, and some might say that as a stubborn individual — and one of life's fighters — she was certainly not going to be the willing victim of a chronic, debilitating condition.

PREFACE

The day before departure

Neither of us was particularly cool, calm, and collected, and there was no reason why we should be. After all, we were about to leave our home for three months to make the trip of a lifetime around the world. We were understandably apprehensive, but above all, we were very excited about the prospect of travelling.

The suitcase had been packed and repacked with, dare I say, military precision. We had travelled many times before, but the preparation for this was proving to be different. I assumed it was because this was the longest journey we would ever undertake, and on this occasion there would be a wheelchair and a walking frame to factor in.

We were by no means new to travelling to far-flung places; we had done this many times, so it should be relatively easy. On previous journeys we had been very good at travelling light, but for some extraordinary reason, this time it was proving harder to achieve. Did I really require twenty-five tops when in his view ten would be adequate? When would a man realize that a woman needs to consider every eventuality that arises and requires the appropriate clothes so she is not taken by surprise? For someone who was normally in touch with his feminine side, he was demonstrating that he was missing the gene only women possessed. Somewhat disgruntled, he eventually crammed everything I had requested into the already bulging suitcase.

INTRODUCTION

I am not a celebrity wishing to put together an autobiography, just your average ordinary girl with a wish to produce a book about a very special journey shared by two people in extraordinary circumstances.

We met when I was twenty and he was thirty-three. We were doing the musical Chicago. Amateur dramatics, whether dancing, acting, or singing, was a passion we shared.

By the time I was twenty-one we were living with each other, and just a few months later we were delivered the news that I had been diagnosed with multiple sclerosis. At that time, the only advice given to us was to have children sooner rather than later if we wanted them. We were at the beginning of our relationship, and children hadn't even been thought of, let alone discussed; it was far too early for that. I didn't even know if David was going to stick around or not. Luckily for me, he did.

We got married when I was twenty-six. We were now in this together, and life continued pretty much as normal; we were having a lot of fun. For many years my health didn't get in the way, and we carried on living life to the fullest. We continued acting, singing, and dancing and playing hockey, and we persevered with improving our skiing abilities. I could lie and say that I was brilliant at all of them, and you would never know, but in reality I was run-of-the-mill, I still loved everything I did.

Without a hint of a warning, when I was thirty-five the course of our lives changed direction completely. The progressive nature of the condition started to rear its ugly head and invade my body, and by 2005 it was necessary for me to give up work. Our lives were about to be taken in an altogether different direction. This was now frightening, unfamiliar, and uncharted territory.

Later that year, we received an invitation for a wedding in Hawaii that would take place in 2006, you might think this was not so special, but it was. We wanted to go to the wedding, and since it was such a long journey, David and I decided to take full advantage of our time available and travel around the world, with me in a wheelchair.

This is not necessarily exciting to a lot of people, but for us it would prove to be one of the biggest challenges of our lives.

Have you ever wondered what it's like to be disabled? Probably not, and I can't say that I blame you. Why should you? Suffice it to say, we all take an awful lot for granted, and it's not until you lose the use of your legs, arms, hands, and strength that you suddenly realize what you had and how precious it was.

I am a young woman who loves life, but sadly I am unable to live it alone. I share my life with my wonderful husband, David. We have a passion and a zest for many things in life, and one great shared passion for travelling.

We spent months planning our itinerary and learned that we had to be very specific about certain requirements. The one thing I was really concerned about was the bathroom facilities, and we were very keen to stress my requirements to the travel agent. It wasn't until we started travelling that we realized just how important it was to be very clear about personal needs. I was soon to be educated about how different the needs of a disabled person could vary from the needs of another disabled person, and it's safe to say we learnt the hard way.

Our journey commenced on 16 January, returning home to the United Kingdom on 20 April, 2006.

I had already decided that whilst we were travelling I would send regular updates of our experiences via e-mail to our friends and family. I would do this for two reasons: first, we could let everybody know what we were up to, and second, I would always have a record of what I had written so it would serve to remind me of just what we had managed to achieve. A few people also sent e-mails back, letting us know what they were up to and what was happening at home, and in some cases there were some very random and indeed funny tales. Receiving e-mails kept us in touch with events at home and helped us to keep our feet firmly planted on the ground. I have chosen to include my e-mails together with some edited responses in order to build a complete picture.

Whilst writing I have tried to highlight the highs and lows that we encountered, never forgetting that there is often a humorous side to most things.

The catalogue of our journey has taken me quite a few years to put together, using one finger to type and voice-recognition software. Whilst travelling I was able to capture my memories and my emotions by using a Dictaphone, so they would be eternally printed in my mind. Emotionally, there were times that the journey was very difficult, and whilst most people would probably keep them to themselves, it is my choice to share, and I feel that it is very important to convey my feelings - the whole truth and nothing but the truth.

I am about to take you on our travels, and I ask you to try and imagine what it is like to travel around the world in a wheelchair.

To my darling David, without whom this journey

and life itself would not be possible.

I thank you.

A guide to our journey

Day One
Flight One, London to Bangkok

"Two drifters off to see the world, there's such a lot
of world to see.
We're after the same rainbow's end…"

"Moon River"
Lyrics by Johnny Mercer

After planning our trip for several months we could scarcely believe the day had finally arrived for us to set off on our journey. I pinched myself and David just for good measure; we were soon to leave the United Kingdom to embark on a trip of a lifetime, circumnavigating the world. It was an unearthly time of the morning, 04.00, which is often referred to as the "death hour." Now I understood why it's called this. It was an extremely cold January morning when my brother-in-law came bounding through the front door to pick us up. He was so annoyingly cheerful at this time of day I felt like I wanted to punch him but thought better of it; after all, he was driving us to the airport, and I was hardly awake.

Our luggage consisted of an extremely large suitcase, a rucksack, our precious computer case which contained all of our travel documentation and a fold-up walking frame, all of which was crammed into the car. Fond farewells,

Nicky Dalladay

hugs, and kisses were liberally exchanged with our bleary-eyed friends, who would be kindly house sitting for the next three months. I was not at all concerned about leaving our home in the hands of our friends, though I had a sneaky suspicion they would undoubtedly set off the burglar alarm several times over the course of the next three months. Sometimes we worried about the strangest things; should the alarm go off, so be it, there would be nothing either of us could do. They would just have to deal with it.

Our journey, like most of the trips we made, began on the M25, which has to be one of the most hideous and overused roads since time began. The traffic had already begun to build, and I was made fully aware that I had two grown men in front of me making noises that we should have left earlier, that as at this rate there would not be enough time to get to the airport. *Don't panic, Mr. Mannering* sprang to mind, and I left them to it. I was supremely confident we would get there on time. I just sat back with a wry smile on my face and let them extol the virtues of their male logic to ensure we would get to our destination of London Heathrow Airport on time. Probably worth pointing out now this husband and wife partnership consisted of one very pessimistic and one very optimistic person, which became evident during the course of the next three months.

Hooray, we arrived at the airport without bloodshed, and whilst the journey admittedly did take longer, it had certainly not taken the four hours either man had anticipated. David always likes to be in good time for everything; this incident was neither the first nor would

My Travels with Wheely

it be the last that we endured.

I had always said we would get there in plenty of time and there was no need to worry, but needless to say, my words weren't acknowledged by either of them. They congratulated themselves in a manly fashion, evidently proud that the first phase of our journey had been executed and accomplished - well done them. Fantastic, we had indeed arrived at the airport, but our flight's scheduled departure time was not until 11.50. Thanks to the navigator and driver, we got there by 06.30. Without wishing to sound ungrateful I looked at the positive: at least it enabled us plenty of time for an extremely leisurely four-hour breakfast! I amused myself by wondering just how much we could tuck away in four hours.

Having arrived in good time, the check-in for our flight was not even open. I suspected that the check-in staff had barely left home yet. *What do we do now?* I wondered. There were a few alternatives I could think of, none of which were particularly inspiring. We could just sit and wait here until the desk opened, or I could slip outside to finish my packet of cigarettes. Bridget Jones entered my thoughts as I seemed to recall she was always on the verge of giving up smoking. With promises made to myself I was going to give up smoking while we were on our travels, I firmly believed I would be successful, but I might as well just finish the packet first. I couldn't bear waste and did not intend to throw them away; that was just plain silly and would be a waste of money. I convinced myself that if I chain smoked enough to make myself feel sick, I would never want to smoke again. This method seemed to work for a lot of people, although

Nicky Dalladay

I cunningly forgot that I had been a smoker for some considerable time, so any thought of failure did not enter my head. Being an optimist, I was certain I would crack the habit and positive I would be successful.

At last, the workforce consisting of one person stationed at her post, ready to receive two very excited travellers. The check-in desk was opened and the little "donkey train" of David, one very large suitcase, a folding walking frame, a rucksack, a computer case, and of course me in "Wheely" made its way over the plush purple carpet of business class. Originally, we had intended to travel economy, but after I considered the enormity of the task that David was going to have to go through felt it would be preferable to upgrade to business class. It seemed only right we should do this.

During the course of my life I have often given names to things for my own amusement. We were not alone in our travels but were accompanied by my wheelchair, which was the recipient of the name "Wheely," and in the general pecking order came after David and before me. I had decided that Wheely was male — rather strange, I know — I am not deranged and do realize a wheelchair is an inanimate object.

When my legs started to give up on me I used a walking stick. Then it got harder it was necessary to use crutches, swiftly followed by a Zimmer frame — whoopee, an instant advancement in age by forty years or so. Finally, the specialists pronounced, rather bluntly I might add, I was an accident waiting to happen. This meant only one thing to me: that it was now necessary for me to use a

My Travels with Wheely

wheelchair. I was horrified that my body had become so useless the only way for me to get around was by being pushed. Emotionally and mentally I fought hard against this. I really didn't want to end up this way; I had been an independent woman for so long and yet I was about to be stripped of this. As hard as it was there was absolutely nothing I could do about it. I would have to dig down deep within myself and accept that a wheelchair would become part of our lives, whether we liked it or not.

The relationship between the two of us has become a very strong bond; one is not much use without the other. Wheely is now very much part of my life and forms who I am as a person; therefore, he deserved to have a name and to be treated with respect. This would be our first major trip abroad with Wheely, and I anticipated there would be all sorts of new boundaries and barriers to overcome, but for the moment I pushed this thought firmly to the back of my mind.

We were deliriously happy. Our dream was soon to become a reality, and we would experience life in many countries and learn about different cultures. Our happiness was temporarily cut short it faded when the woman responsible for issuing the tickets barely gave us a second glance. Didn't she realize what we were about to do? She asked David for our passports in a monosyllabic tone and tapped the keys of her computer, directing all questions to David; she didn't acknowledge that I was even there. How quickly it reminded me that I ran the risk of losing my identity by becoming a third-class citizen, but no, I wasn't going to let that happen; this was now the twenty-first century, and I made a note not to

Nicky Dalladay

let this episode upset me. This was only day one, and if I didn't toughen up now, how would I manage for the next three months? I had no idea what her name was, and to be honest I didn't really care; to make myself feel better, in my mind I called her "Ms. Glum." She certainly had the face to go with it.

The luggage allowance was 32kg per person, not including the frame and Wheely, which were thankfully excluded. We felt fairly smug and safe in the knowledge we had just one — albeit it — very large and heavy suitcase for the two of us, and we were in the full belief that we were travelling light. We had rather cleverly worked out, well we thought, that this must equal 64kg between us, irrespective of how many cases this was spread over, and we only had the one case. Wrong. It was per item of luggage, and there was absolutely no flexibility on this and certainly no consideration extended to David, who had to cart the donkey train around for the next three months or so. Our suitcase weighed in at 34.5kg. Surely this must be acceptable; a curt *no* confirmed it was most definitely not. What a great start! We had to unpack 2.5kg there and then and spend the next five minutes trying to agree on what should be relocated and shoved into the already heaving rucksack.

An orange Thai Airways label marked "heavy" appeared for the bag, and Ms. Glum proceeded to attach it to our suitcase with great flourish. We hadn't even bought anything yet but had managed to use up our entire baggage allowance. How were we going to manage for the duration of our journey? Ms. Glum spoke and wished us a pleasant flight, any form of sincerity completely

My Travels with Wheely

missing from her brief utterance. The remainder of the donkey train departed, and without further ado we made our way straight to the business class lounge for what was by now a much-needed breakfast.

I had just spotted a smoking lounge. Actually it resembled a smoke-filled chamber. I asked David to park Wheely and me there just so I could finish my packet of cigarettes. Nearly done, I had only one left. I congratulated myself. I was very nearly an ex-smoker.

They had great Internet access at Heathrow, and thanks to our extremely early arrival at the airport, I had plenty of time to update our e-mail mailing list. I composed our first brief e-mail message and sent it off. *Who knows?* I thought. We might even get some replies.

First E-mail
Day One of some ninety-odd days to go

Well we got here, Heathrow, perhaps a little earlier than expected, and we are in the lounge — business class, of course. We cannot tell you how excited we are so far, and we haven't even managed to pass first base! This is a test more than anything to see if we managed to set the e-mail group up correctly. Could someone please (I have to take the risk that it could be all of you) just confirm you got this. Very big thanks for all of your lovely e-mail messages, text messages, cards, letters, and phone calls to wish us bon voyage; it was much appreciated. We shall think of you all often and miss you all dreadfully. Trying hard to think of a suitable sign-off name for ourselves, so if you have any suggestions please let us know.

With much love
Nicky & David
xxxx

Just as I thought, we had so much time on our hands that we were able to read all of the response messages immediately and pondered over the sign-off suggestions.

E-mails Received

Wow, Heathrow, what about Holidays as a sign off? NB.

Travelling Dalladays? P &CF.

How about DallAwayDays? AC.

What about the Dynamic Duo or Holidays? GH.

I still think you should be the Holidays, I am missing you already. JMB.

Dear Mad Birds, best of luck for the trip of a lifetime. LE.

How about Dilly Dally? RA.

Great to hear you've got there (Heathrow). What about Lou & Andy? LA.

Good on you both. AA

Wow, fantastic! Bon Voyage, Intrepids (how's that for a name?). I can't wait for the next instalment. MH.

My Travels with Wheely

Already miss you. Didn't set off the alarm today! Have a fantastic time. MK.

How about the Traveldays? AM.

Enjoy your trip, you deserve it. PW.

I'm sure that Heathrow Airport has to be more riveting than work, enjoy and Bon Voyage! CB.

Have a ball, and more importantly, enjoy your trip of a lifetime! DJ.

I can't wait to hear of your travels as you get nearer to Hawaii. I am looking forward to catching up. CJK.

We shall keep track of you whereabouts. Enjoy authentic Thai Cuisine. R&GD.

Received loud and clear. Have a fantastic time. KS.

Received and looking forward to all of your bulletins. TJ.

I will endeavour to think of unique name if possible. MG.

The first thing that I thought of was you two when I woke up this morning. Have a wonderful time. EM.

Hi you two, got it. Love ya. S&GM.

We would have to give a little thought to the suggestions.

Having upgraded to business class we found ourselves in the position of having to make the first major decision

Nicky Dalladay

of the trip. We were actually asked, yes asked, if we would like to board the plane first or last. Do you know? I had never had this question posed to me before. In steerage class I was put on first and taken off last, that was the deal, no negotiation whatsoever. David left me with the task of making this very important choice. First or last, what should we opt for? It seemed an eternity whilst I weighed up the pros and cons; dithering in this fashion was usually reserved exclusively for David. Finally, I settled for first, as it was my understanding in business class you were offered drinks while the rest of the plane boarded. Any well-seasoned traveller who went by business class would have known this automatically; luckily I got there in the end. Boy, did we feel like a drink; after all, we had been up for several hours, the sun must surely be over the yardarm by now?

We were politely asked to board the plane; evidentially flummoxed by this form of treatment I decided that one could become quite accustomed to this way of life. I wanted to go to the toilet again, although somewhat surprised there was anything left to come out. This was the last chance I had to go before leaving U.K. soil; I'm comfortable going to the lavatory in this country because we had a procedure and knew exactly what most of the facilities were like and what was available for me. Suddenly, panic fell over me. What were the toilet facilities like in other countries? I realized this probably was not most people's thought before going away, but it just so happened it was mine at this particular moment. I felt sick with fear. Why were we doing this? Had I really considered what David was going to have to go through? Admittedly, whilst I felt excited on one hand

My Travels with Wheely

I felt nervous on the other, and I was certain David felt the same; strangely, neither of us uttered a word of this to each other.

At the aircraft door I transferred to an aisle chair, which was very narrow, barely accommodating the width of my posterior. I took a final look at Wheely, who then disappeared; he would have to travel in the hold. I vacated the chair, and with alarm I was now informed business class was situated upstairs. This was a "tiny detail" the dispassionate and unhelpful Ms. Glum failed to mention. Metaphorically, my climbing head needed to be firmly placed on before the expedition was able to commence. The carcass of my body needed to get up there somehow.

I hauled myself up whilst David lifted my feet up one by one up each step; it was not a pretty sight. By the time I got to the top I was drenched in sweat and totally exhausted. I must be one of the strangest people I know as thoughts trickled into my head. I was thankful I was wearing trousers. How ridiculous, as I rarely wear anything but trousers. Nonetheless, I was still relieved I was not wearing a skirt as should I fall over there would be no loss of dignity on this occasion. I dragged my feet along the aisle, holding on to anything I could find to help me, be it somebody's head, shoulder, arm, or any bodily part, basically anything that enabled me to get to my seat. As the slow journey continued, I noticed just how large the seats were; maybe we would have to share one? Or did we have one each? David helped me into my seat on the aisle side, allowing him the window that he loves, mainly because he always provides me with a

Nicky Dalladay

running commentary of the ground and cloud formation, whether I'm interested or not.

We snuggled into our huge seats and were asked what we would like to drink. No problem with this one, and we decided champagne was the only drink for us right now; we toasted each other and kissed. We sat back and relaxed, nonchalantly flicking through the menus and sipping our champagne whilst economy were still boarding. This was the life. How decadent we felt, totally immersed in our own thoughts. But there was an air of anxious tension between us. Trepidation set in. Would we be all right? What happened if our carefully laid plans backfired? What if we didn't get on? What if …? and so on. It was too late for second thoughts. The plane took off, and David began his running commentary.

The plane journey was truly awful and just seemed to go on forever. Well, it actually took ten and a half hours, to be precise. My body managed to have involuntary leg spasms for the duration of the flight, which at first can seem quite funny, I have learned that a sense of humour can help, but then it got nasty. The "alien" that occupies my body decided I would not have a pleasant journey. Ms. Glum popped into my thoughts once again. She was the one who had wished us a pleasant journey. How it annoyed me that this phrase was handed out with gay abandon before you got on the plane; this gesture seemed somewhat futile and ironic at this moment. The alien had clearly decided otherwise, and I found myself at the mercy of what my body intended to do without my permission. Rather than having the pleasant flight I was offered by Ms. Glum, I was the recipient of the

My Travels with Wheely

most unpleasant flight I had ever experienced. The alien put me through the most horrific level of painful spasms for most of the journey; they just wouldn't go away. If only I could detach my legs and hang them up for the remainder of the flight. At that moment I felt this trip was not one my better ideas. I just wanted to cry and go home, a fact I concealed from David.

Talk about fed-up. This was not the way our amazing journey should start. It must surely only get better from here on in. Just how wrong could I possibly be? Luckily we were both wearing T-shirts; it was sweltering and very uncomfortable. Aeroplanes are either hot or cold; seemingly they don't do that crucial in-between bit; my thoughts drifted rather randomly. I was reminded that hospitals were always hot. There was something waiting in the wings to enter the stage; I felt its presence. Another different alien reared its head, and suddenly both of us showed signs of colds. What a start! All we wanted at this moment was to crawl into our comfortable bed at home, but this was not an option. Again, Bridget Jones entered my thoughts; I don't recall her having had such a miserable time.

Day Two
Bangkok

Hooray! Our dream finally became a reality. The plane landed, and we could at last get off. Bemused, knackered, and plagued with germs courtesy of the airline, we were met at the airport by a charming gentleman. He welcomed us to his country and informed us Bangkok was the main gateway to the Orient.

It was early in the morning when we arrived in downtown Bangkok, or should I say, as informed by our ever so cheery driver, the City of Angels. I decided, having been a cheerful person in the morning, I now found I was somewhat grumpy; I would have to put it down to the lack of sleep.

We transferred to the car and were instantly overwhelmed by the strong smell of something like incense and the collection of Buddha's that occupied any free space in the car. Oblivious to our exhaustion, our charming gentleman driver felt sure we required some background information, clearly unaware both his passengers were nodding off in the back of the car. For some extraordinary reason, I recalled him saying the Thai people didn't actually call their capital city by the name we used; they actually called it Krung Thep, which roughly translated to the City of Angels, and unbeknownst to me, apparently it was also known worldwide by this name. Why didn't people stick to one name? Life was confusing

My Travels with Wheely

enough, but does a variety of names really matter? No, of course it doesn't.

It was now 07.30, and Bangkok had come alive with people trying to get to work. We temporarily emerged from our weary state to witness pandemonium everywhere we were, being well and truly welcomed by the hustle and bustle of everyday life in Bangkok. The cars, bikes, tuk-tuks, and pedestrians created havoc trying to get to their destinations.

I was reminded immediately we were no longer in the United Kingdom but in a country which had very different rules from ours; perhaps it would be more accurate to say it looked like they didn't have any rules at all. I had never witnessed this level of chaos on such a grand scale before. It was a miracle we didn't see a fatal accident or at the very least a punch up. By no means did I wish to sound unkind, but I was relieved, as apparently we were nearly there; he had been a very charming gentleman but unable to realize his passengers didn't really want the guided tour just yet.

Finally, we were deposited at our hotel, the Sheraton Grande Sukhumvit. The alien spasms that had controlled my body earlier had now dissipated, much to my relief. The hotel looked bright, airy, and very welcoming. We decided we should be more than happy with this as a base for the next few days. David went to the reception clutching our passports and voucher to check us in to our new home for the next three nights. I on the other hand had discovered I had one remaining cigarette, and seemingly forgetting I was actually an ex smoker of twelve

Nicky Dalladay

hours or so, I lit it up and enjoyed it.

To say we both felt rather disoriented and not quite knowing what to do with ourselves was a bit of an understatement. What should we be doing getting up, going to bed, eating? We were now in a different time zone and really didn't know what to do, but one thing was certain, we were both extremely tired. Utterly exhausted, we decided sleep was what we really needed and went to bed for a couple of hours. But we did set an alarm clock just so we didn't freak our bodies out too much. We wanted to ration ourselves, so we ensured we would get up and didn't waste the first day of our adventure. It seemed as though we had only just dropped off into a deep sleep when the alarm woke us with some dreadful noise. It went off at noon, and we struggled very hard to prize our eyes apart and wake up. This was not easy; we had both slept very heavily.

Eventually, we managed to get up and noticed our room for the first time; it was a lovely large area that was beautifully furnished. The bathroom was fabulous and had a walk-in shower, which instantly reassured me that this was how it would be for the duration of our trip. I congratulated myself that my persistence in reiterating our requirements when booking had actually paid off, clever me. I leapt, well, maybe not leapt, but rather lurched into the shower. The warm water flowed down our backs. It was relaxing and helped us unwind; we felt fresh and clean once more. We finished our shower, changed into clean clothes, and immediately felt revitalised and raring to go again.

My Travels with Wheely

Amazingly enough, within no time at all we had pretty much forgotten the epic journey of the previous night. Rather oddly, we hadn't bothered to count the number of flights we would have to make, and with just one flight down we casually wondered how many more there were to go. We glanced at the enormous computer bag with our tickets and realized there were many more yet to come. Better not to think about that one too much; we would deal with each one as it happened. We decided to treat each day as though it was our last and savour every moment as each new experience unfolded.

There was just one thing I needed to do before we could go out, and that was to make a local telephone call. Yes, we had a friend in Bangkok, Krung Thep, the City of Angels, or whatever you wanted to call it. When I say friend, this was not strictly accurate. Let me explain. Prior to us leaving London we were put in touch with a lady called Maureen who goes to Bangkok annually for three months and thought it would be nice to meet up with her. I suppose it would in a funny way, but we had only been away from home for a little over twenty-four hours, so it wasn't like we needed to see someone from home just yet. Having telephoned her to establish contact whilst still in London, we arranged I would call her again on arrival, and this was what I was about to do. We chatted briefly, and because of her full diary it turned out the only night she was free to meet us was tonight. Bang went the myth that octogenarians led sedate and depleted lifestyles. We arranged to meet her in the lobby of our hotel at 19.00, hoping we would still be awake.

By now it was well into the afternoon, and we decided

Nicky Dalladay

to venture out for some fresh air and see what sights we could squeeze in during our couple of days in Bangkok. Why only a few days? This stop was only ever intended to be used for a rest period after the long flight from London and to set us up for our hectic schedule in Vietnam. Without a care in the world, we left the hotel without a map. Should we go left or right? We might just as well have tossed a coin, what did we know? Right it was, and we wandered along the crumbling pavements of the enormous Sukhumvit Road in the intense heat. My goodness it was hot.

The roads were more than a little chaotic; nobody took a blind bit of notice of people crossing the road even though they were doing it at the correct place and at the appointed moment. They didn't honour any road signs or speed controls; they were all quite mad and seemed to have some sort of death wish. They have conditioned themselves to beep their horns continuously on cars and motor bikes alike for no apparent reason other than to increase the noise pollution. I mentioned we were stepping out for some fresh air, but it turned out there wasn't any. I honestly didn't think we had been anywhere as polluted with such grime, noise, and crowds before. I would perfectly understand if you got the wrong impression that I wasn't enamoured, but in an odd way, this place was strangely alluring. I didn't quite know why; perhaps it would become clear in a few days.

With the pavement crumbling beneath foot, and Wheely of course, we bravely soldiered on. Needless to say, it just got worse. We happened upon the BTS Skytrain and thought this was a good idea; that was when we managed

My Travels with Wheely

to work out how to get up to the platform. The Skytrain is allegedly fast, safe, and very reliable. Sounded good enough to us, and of course it offered the added bonus that we got to avoid the traffic, tuk-tuks, people, and pollution. We located the disabled passenger lift and tried to fathom out just how it worked. It wasn't easy, but at last we were successful in completing this arduous task. Now where was the ticket office? If only we were linguists we could read the signs in Thai. Sadly, neither of us possesses such fine skills, so we settled for the international waving of arms and pointing to the map in the lobby trying to explain where it was we wanted to go to. Sorted, it seemed to have worked, not quite sure how, but it had, and David parted with some Thai Bhats and returned with one ticket. We were a little confused, but it would seem I got to travel for nothing. It appeared there was an upside to being disabled. You get to save some money, 20p in this case; I suppose it's the thought that counts, as they certainly didn't have to do it.

The journey on the Skytrain was soon to commence. We found ourselves being escorted to the platform which, to say the least, was strange as it was next to the ticket office, so even we could have found it. With the use of the supplied map we had worked out we would need to change trains, but our newly acquired escort was trying to tell us something. It was no good; we just didn't understand what he was trying to say. We waved goodbye to him but remained somewhat puzzled. All of the railway staff we met were extremely polite and helpful. The Thais are such lovely people, but I couldn't help wondering what he was trying to let us know from the other side of the glass.

Nicky Dalladay

Once boarded, we watched for names of the stations and tried to work out where we had to alight. Success — we arrived at Siam station. As the doors opened we were very surprised to be greeted by a member of staff who guided us toward a set of stairs. My heart sank. We obviously needed to go up to change trains, but I couldn't climb this mountain. There was clearly no disabled lift to take me to the next platform, so how did they expect me to get up there? Before we had time to utter a word, the solution was in front us. Four tiny Thai men, members of staff, lifted me up in Wheely. Fear overwhelmed me. They really were going to carry me up the stairs. Did they realize how much I weighed? They got me to the top in one piece, and they were drenched in sweat, which didn't surprise me in the least. I had never had an experience quite like this before. There we had it, safely transported, and we could now change trains. With a lot of hand gesturing we thanked everybody profusely and bade them farewell. Oh no, we were back where we had started — they seemed to be trying to tell us something. Not again! We didn't understand them the first time; didn't they know we were stupid Brits?

We arrived at our station, Saphan Taksin. The train doors opened and again, there was another person to escort us, although we were not really sure why, surely we could find our way out of the building; after all, we are grownups. Ah, but then again, confronting us there was a "mother" of a staircase we would never get down. Proven wrong once again, which is often the case, four tiny Thai men emerged, picked me up, and carried me and Wheely down. It was incredibly steep and scary looking down the stairs; I was elevated to such heights that I wondered how

My Travels with Wheely

this differed from riding in a sedan chair. With delusions of grandeur, I decided I rather liked this form of travel. Was there a chance this would catch on in London? I wondered. Had a similar situation occurred in the United Kingdom I would have been made to feel like a nuisance, and David and I would have to manage alone. Much to our relief, Bangkok appeared not to be governed by health and safety issues, and I hoped they would not lose their spirit; they were exceptional people.

Safely out of the building, and three of our helpers disappeared, but one remained and continued to push me toward the Chao Phraya River. He had correctly worked out that the reason for us being there was to take a cruise up the river. He even assisted us with the purchase of tickets and a bottle of water, and then poof! He was off like a genie. We gave no consideration as to how we would manage to board the boat; this was just a minor detail. If you spent time thinking about these little obstacles, you wouldn't do anything. Once again, there were more willing helpers who gathered around us, and without the need of gesturing they lifted me onto the boat. What would we have done without the help of all these people? We were truly grateful.

The Chao Phraya River appears to play many roles in Thai life, and it is even regarded as the principal artery of the nation. As it flows, the river carries with it the history and the culture of the country, once dubbed the Venice of the East. We cruised slowly up the river and were rewarded with many beautiful sights. Our fellow passengers were a little intrigued and kept looking at us, so I smiled, and they smiled back; in fact, there was a lot

21

Nicky Dalladay

of smiling on that trip. We mainly saw temples and had a glimpse of the Grand Palace. It was very peaceful on the river; the hustle and bustle of the city seemed a long time ago. The trip lasted for about an hour and gave us a good opportunity to see some of the most fabulous buildings. It was well worth the journey as it gave us another flavour of Bangkok. We were so hot and our clothes just stuck to us, and we needed to buy more bottles of water.

Once again, we received more help getting me off the boat. These petite, gentle people, who looked as though they couldn't pick up a piece of paper, deftly scooped me up and away we went. Not quite certain how we were going to get back into the train station, and before we could even give it a second thought, a smiling man appeared. It was the same man who had escorted us to the river. He took control and pushed me around to the other side of the building whilst a bemused David trotted behind. Once more we were completely in his hands, and we trusted him implicitly. Around the other side of the building we now saw that it housed an escalator. He radioed for some colleagues; I assumed that was what he was doing, as three other men suddenly appeared. Wheely, the modern day sedan chair, and its occupant were elevated once more, and up we both went, being delivered safely to the platform. We encountered the same procedure on the way back to the hotel, and a man appeared whenever we were getting off the train in exactly the right location; they were obviously radioing ahead. Thinking about this much later, we could of course have made this journey by taxi but it never once occurred to us to do that, and I was rather glad we didn't.

My Travels with Wheely

We had just experienced human nature at its very best, which was a wonderful feeling. I was not made to feel an inconvenience once. These kind people facilitated my needs at that time, and they wanted nothing in return, other than a smile. I was convinced that had we been elsewhere in the world there would have been a few outstretched palms. Just goes to show what a cynical individual life has made me. In my opinion, they went above and beyond the call of duty. What amazing people they were. Was this a good omen for the rest of our trip? We would have to wait and see.

As we approached the hotel we came across a street market and found ourselves purchasing another travel bag, a very small one. This purchase on day one served to prove it was nonsense that we would be travelling light for the next three months. We would now be travelling much heavier than intended, and it looked like the donkey train just got bigger. I own up and take full responsibility for this "gaff" as it was largely down to yours truly and her many tops she wished to take.

Back at the hotel I had another local call to make. Bizarrely an old colleague of mine was on business in Bangkok. I called him and arranged to meet for dinner tomorrow night. It seemed as though our social life was on the up, and it wasn't this good at home. We freshened up and got ready to meet for the prearranged drink. I suspected it would be an early night; after all, she was eighty-five.

We met up and headed straight for the bar. She was indeed very sprightly for her years and made me feel about ninety-five — there was no justice. We ordered a round of gin and tonics, demonstrating just how British we were, when I noticed there were people smoking in the bar. I asked the waiter for a packet of cigarettes. David looked at me but said nothing. I felt the need to retort that I shall give them up when we were in Vietnam, and I meant it. It was a marvellous evening. We were thoroughly entertained by this lady of advancing years. I stifled a yawn and glanced at my watch to see it was now 00.30. Our newfound friend jumped to her feet and said, "You must be tired." How right she was. I was under the impression that old people went to bed early, but again, how wrong could I be?

Today had been an extremely long day, and it had been without a shadow of doubt a truly magnificent and very memorable one.

I was so happy I could burst.

E-mail Received

For the life of me I can't remember when you said you were going. I hope you both have a safe and exciting trip. RH.

He obviously didn't receive our first e-mail message or just forgot; I must make sure he's on our list.

Day Three

Our charming gentleman, who picked us up from the airport, arrived to escort us from the hotel in a chauffeur-driven car. He shook our hands and greeted us warmly, but he was soft spoken, and we struggled to hear what he said. His hair was very dark and slicked back with gel, as was the chauffeur's. The car had the odour of stale incense and every surface was again occupied by Buddha's.

Yesterday we booked this trip to visit the Damnoen Saduak Floating Market, as every tourist should. The market lies 110km Southwest of Bangkok and the drive along the dilapidated roads ensured that this relatively short journey turned out to be a long one. En route we were taken to a craft centre on the pretext of stopping for a toilet break. We had to get out of the car whether we wanted to or not to watch the locals hard at work grinding down some coconut into sugar, we were informed. Two giggling old toothless women proffered an unappetising leaf with a mess of brown sugar on it in our direction. They actually wanted us to eat it. Cautiously we tried it. It was delicious and reminded me of Cornish fudge. I doubted this was low in calories.

The craft centre was full of beautiful, vibrantly coloured orchids, which apparently grew in Thailand like weeds; oh, they were so lucky; I adore them. There was the obligatory shopping area for us to pass through where you could buy all sorts of rubbish — sorry, I meant to say

Nicky Dalladay

treasured, high-quality goods. In spite of people pushing their wares right under our noses, we managed to avoid falling into their trap and parting with any money.

We continued our journey toward the market on this very hot and sticky day. The car was air conditioned but we continued to sweat. Our charming gentleman suggested we open the windows for some breeze as an alternative. Finally, we arrived at the Damnoen Saduk floating market and were not disappointed. It was amazingly spectacular and buzzing with life; not a bad reaction from two people who hate markets.

We walked by the river to predominantly see old women selling fruits and vegetables from their boats. We took an awful lot of pictures. There was so much to see and the colour and vibrancy was just wonderful. There were many scenes, each depicting its own individual story. David managed to capture the most fantastic photograph I had ever seen of an elderly woman in her boat selling the most appetising fruit. It was very hard to guess just how old she actually was, but I suspected she was not as old as I thought; her life was evidently a hard one and not helped by the sun damage I'm sure she must have encountered. Generally, life there appeared to be simplistic and certainly not what we were used to.

When we need shopping, of course we go to the local supermarket. We purchase food that has been treated with so many chemicals that to us it looks perfect. Here it was very different. The fruit and vegetables had a natural, unhampered look about them. I can't say they had the same appeal, but they do have a superior taste.

My Travels with Wheely

Our charming gentleman kindly bought us some fruit to try — something with a very pale lemon colour and taste vaguely like that of a grapefruit. The fresh flavours exploded in your mouth. It was gorgeous.

Right beside the floating market there was a covered market, and naturally we found ourselves being herded toward it. *Interesting,* I thought. The entrance was accessed via a dubious piece of wood plank, and it was quite obvious the market was heaving with people. With help, we managed to get up the plank and into the market. At the doorway there was an old woman haranguing everybody who passed, and she shoved every conceivable trinket you could think of under their nose trying to make a sale. All of a sudden she spotted us. *Oh god*, I thought. She was heading in our direction and could see I was a sitting target and was unlikely to let us go until we bought something. I was wrong. Instead, she threw her hands in the air, made lots of noise, and parted the crowds to enable us to continue on our way. Once we were safely out of the way, she continued where she had left off and harangued the crowds.

On our journey back we made a stop to go the toilet, and we found ourselves at another Thai craft centre. This time we watched some woodcarving being done, which was quite incredible watching the skilful workers use their tools with such precision and respect. We successfully avoided another buying opportunity; we would have to carry on being strong about this. We chose not to buy for the simple reason we had three months ahead of us on the road with no spare luggage space.

Nicky Dalladay

We climbed back into the car with all its Buddha's and very strange aromas, which by now were becoming quite unpleasant — a sweet smell combined with a stale body odour. We believed this was the last stop and were on our way back to the hotel. Just minutes later we stopped again. Surely this was not another toilet stop. We had only just been! No, you guessed it — another craft centre. In reality, we didn't really mind, they were just trying to make a living, and who can blame them? Oh well, we would just have to remember they were trying to boost their economy. Keep smiling but not buying.

The end of this trip was nigh, but just when you thought it was safe, you found yourself passing through Bangkok's most dangerous street market. Why so? There was a railway line going right through the middle of it. The market traders had to leap to safety and out of the way when a train was coming. There really were no health and safety issues in existence here; I loved it.

The side streets of Bangkok were awash with private enterprise. People were making a living using a sewing machine to mend or make clothes, while others were hairdressers with some who groomed men with a cutthroat razor. Whilst Sweeney Todd came to mind, I did admire their ingenuity and skill.

Back at the hotel we enjoyed a light lunch and talked about the events of the morning before heading off to enjoy a stroll, taking in the chaos on the roads of downtown Bangkok. We passed a backstreet massage parlour, and I decided I wanted to go for a foot and leg massage. This was most definitely not for self-indulgent

My Travels with Wheely

pampering reasons but in the hope it would attempt to reduce the swelling in my ankles. They had swollen to such proportions they looked like they belonged to an elephant and looked fairly hideous.

With David's help I entered the tiny parlour, which was no larger than six feet by five feet. Yet they had been extremely creative and used the small area to squeeze five beds in; there was literally no room to swing a cat. Now that we were in this minute room, there was just the matter of the language barrier to overcome. We pointed at the poster outside and indicated I'd like to have a foot and leg massage. I settled into one of the treatment chairs and waited. I looked up and saw five Thai girls staring at me; they were so young and looked as though they should still be at school.

The massage treatment began and started very well and was as I anticipated extremely relaxing. Then, the alien staged a comeback, and both my legs went into uncontrollable spasms. There was nothing I could do apart from watch them shoot out in different directions and nearly kick my masseur in the face. I tried to explain what was happening but it was useless. I was unable to communicate in their language, and they didn't understand me. Instead I giggled nervously. I felt so sorry for the young things who were taken completely by surprise by my performing legs. From their reaction they quite clearly had not seen anything like it before; I wondered what must be going through their minds and doubted they had any idea about my condition. I was very embarrassed by this and felt like a circus act, but it was completely out of my hands. We paid and left the

Nicky Dalladay

parlour.

My ankles were still very swollen and now my legs had erupted with red bumps. What was going on? I'm normally such a healthy person, and now I found very strange things happening to me.

Our sightseeing had to be temporarily put on hold. We needed to find a chemist to see if there was anything to help me. I was not feeling sorry for myself by any means, but I was starting to feel fat, lumpy, and very ugly, so something needed to be done quickly. We continued to wend our way up the streets of Bangkok and saw a chemist, luckily for us, displaying the international green cross symbol. Great, we said, but as we approached the chemist we could see that the way in was via an enormous staircase. This demonstrated just how quickly your spirits can change — one minute great, and in a flash, not so great. We sat at the bottom of the steps and contemplated what we should do. Should David go in and try and explain what was wrong with me and hope for the best? Somehow we felt there was a flaw in that plan, that it just wasn't going to work. Then the unexpected happened. A security guard who had obviously been watching us came down the steps and proceeded to use the international sign language — hand signals accompanied by the waving of arms — and he and David carried me up the steps. We were extremely grateful; there was something so special about the people we were meeting. We were very fortunate.

Now that we were up the steps we were able to go into the chemist and attempt to speak to a pharmacist.

My Travels with Wheely

This was not going to be as easy as we thought. Not quite sure why, but we expected her to speak English, and she didn't. We had fallen into the trap that we thought the world over spoke English, because after all, we as a nation are notoriously bad at speaking languages. Anyway, back to the problem in hand — fat, lumpy, and ugly. The pharmacist looked at me, and I imagined she retreated back a little, as if I was contagious. With a lot of talk that clearly we were never going to understand, we settled on purchasing some drugs we thought were a form of antihistamine pills.

Outside and the lovely security guard reappeared, who was on hand again to assist David to take me down the steps; we were utterly amazed. We were yet to see another person in a wheelchair, so I imagined disabled people were scarce or were locked away somewhere, yet I had been treated as a normal human being. They seemed to instinctively know what to do. I realize how awful that statement is. I am a normal human being. It just so happens that I reside in a wheelchair, but society has a canny way of making me feel abnormal, or perhaps it is just me being paranoid.

Tonight we were meeting my friend and old work colleague, David, for dinner. I found this a little surreal that we would be seeing him here in Bangkok. He was here on business for a few days, and it would be fun to see him. I decided to make a bit of an effort by wearing a skirt and donning some mascara just to prove I could do the feminine thing and dress up; after all, we were likely to be going somewhere smart. Besides, I could at least justify some of my wardrobe that had accompanied us on

Nicky Dalladay

our trip. Blimey, it was only day three and I was already justifying myself. Mental note: *don't do it again.*

He received a recommendation from a colleague in Bangkok for a good restaurant for dinner and we met him there, which was just a short taxi ride from our hotel. The restaurant was beautiful, and because of the warm evening we chose to eat outside. There were a lot of tables with fresh orchids and candles on them. It was such a wonderful setting, only slightly marred by the lack of light to read the menu. We ordered gin and tonics and all selected fish for the main course. It was hard to imagine we were a stone's throw away from the busy main road and total chaos of Bangkok. Equally, it was hard to comprehend the fact there could be somewhere so lovely in the vicinity of this dirty place. We had a great evening. It was easy as we just chatted and laughed whilst trying to see what we were eating in the rather subdued lighting. We said goodbye and looked forward to seeing him in London in some three months' time. It was such a warm evening we decided to walk back to the hotel, as it was easier than getting a taxi.

There was a distinct change in my mood. Tonight I became acutely aware of just how totally dependent I had become. It filled me with horror and grief to see what David had to do for me, or rather us, as a couple. How could I have been so stupid and thoughtless? We were only at the beginning of our journey, and I was already worried about how I was feeling now. We still had some ninety or so days to go. I was not sure we fully realized the extent he would have to help me, which led me to think we were seeing everything through rose-coloured

My Travels with Wheely

glasses. I could only hope as we continued our travels things would not be problematic, that the roads we were yet to go along would not resemble the black hole of Calcutta and life would get a little easier for both of us.

David put me to bed, and I cried myself to sleep.

Day Four

Determined to put my sadness of last night aside, I put my "everything's all right" face on. This face is often worn to mask my real feelings; it is a defence mechanism. With renewed vigour we headed for the Grand Palace, and instead of doing our normal walking everywhere, we decided to take a taxi. I couldn't bear to see those Thai men carry me up and down the steps again. Anyway, they were probably still trying to recover from the injury I caused them. The taxi ride was very exciting around the colourful streets of Bangkok, uncertain if we would get to our destination alive. We held onto the seat belts firmly and leant into the corners with the car. All the motorists tooted their horns, shouted, and made rude gestures to each other. Life was very lively here and observing people was a great pastime. The journey to the Palace took a long time, but not because of the distance but the traffic, which was appalling in Bangkok.

We finally arrived at the Grand Palace, thankfully alive and in one piece. The Grand Palace complex was enormous, and we were quite taken aback by the scale. Our taxi driver dropped us off near the entrance, and we tried to find where to get tickets, which was not obvious. We eventually found a place to purchase tickets and suddenly I roared with laughter. Next to the office was an array of makeshift wheelchairs, which resembled school dining room chairs with wheels and a bar on, resourceful and ingenious in one way but very basic in another. We

My Travels with Wheely

really do take everything we have for granted. I'd love to have seen someone attempt to use one of these chairs. It would be absolutely priceless — but preferably not with me in it. Then it made me feel lucky that our society accommodates people in wheelchairs, more so now than ever before.

Strolling toward the Palace we were pounced on by a very sweet "dumpy" Thai woman. This was very unusual as the people here that we had seen so far were very petite. She appeared to be determined not to let a possible "meal ticket" pass her by and informed us that she would guide us through the Palace so we would be sure not to miss anything. Benefiting from a university education, her English was very good but her words were delivered fast and furiously, and we struggled to keep up. Dumpy had learnt her script very well; so much so that she reeled off all the information she felt we needed to know in order to make our trip a memorable one.

The Grand Palace houses not only the royal residence and throne halls but a number of government offices, as well as the renowned temple of the Emerald Buddha. Dumpy rattled off this information with great enthusiasm. I had a sneaky feeling she did it as quickly as possible so she could get another guided tour under her belt as soon as possible. She proceeded to give us a whirlwind tour of the Grand Palace; believe me, it was certainly fast. We saw the most fabulous buildings decorated in beautiful bright gold, blue, and green. It was too much to take in on one short visit; there was an abundance of everything everywhere you turned. We only paused for breath when she instructed us to take pictures. Did we really want to

Nicky Dalladay

take photographs with various people in the background? But for fear of offending we just did as we were told and took lots of pictures. That's the great thing about a digital camera. You needn't offend anyone; just delete the pictures in the privacy of your hotel.

The Palace is a wonderful tourist attraction and well worth a visit. The Grand Palace is aptly named and covers an area of some 218,000 metres dating back to 1782; luckily we weren't "route marched" through the whole area; we didn't have enough time. Allowing ourselves the briefest of time to visit Bangkok, we had no time left for sightseeing. It was a shame we didn't have more time to spare, I would have liked to have experienced a few more days of mayhem; we were due to leave Bangkok tomorrow for the next leg of our journey.

Day Five
Flight Two, Bangkok to Vietnam

This morning was a very early start and we were up at 04.30. This was such a hard time to get up and even harder to be cheerful. Packed and ready to leave this beautiful hotel we were picked up by our charming gentleman, who was going to transfer us from the hotel to the airport for our flight to Hanoi. This felt like we were starting the whole journey all over again, and now that we were wide awake, we felt excited and very nervous. We had wanted to go to Vietnam for a long time, but I worried that the disabled facilities were going to be nonexistent. We checked in at the airport and before we knew it, we boarded and were ready for takeoff.

At Hanoi airport we were met by our guide, who introduced himself as Hien, which I since understands means nice, kind, and gentle. He smiled a warm hello and welcomed us to Vietnam. He was petite and pleasant to look at but had the most extraordinary set of teeth — they were all crooked and overlapped each other; a visit to the orthodontist would have straightened them out. My gaze moved from his teeth toward his hands. I was intrigued by his very long and beautiful well-manicured nails. Does he play the guitar? I wondered. We were ushered toward a people carrier for our journey, and after a short while of negotiation worked out the best way for me to get into the vehicle. Our guide and driver

Nicky Dalladay

looked on in wonderment, and from their expressions we deduced they were not used to disabled people. At this stage, my feelings were of excitement, and I dismissed any thoughts of negativity that may come my way whilst in Vietnam.

We arrived at the hotel, which was just stunning and not what we were expecting. The building was French colonial style and exuded grandeur and elegance. Our room wasn't ready, and we were invited to have a coffee on the terrace whilst we waited. Outside at the bar the weather was very gloomy and overcast. We pinched ourselves not quite believing we were in Vietnam; another dream had been fulfilled.

At last, our room was ready and we were shown to, it but horror of horrors David informed me that it had a bath with a shower in it. We were lulled into a false sense of security by the wonderful room in Bangkok, with its huge walk-in shower, and we assumed every room would be the same. We tried to explain why it was not possible for us to stay in it, but the woman who had shown it to us didn't understand; unsure of what to do we left the room. I tried hard not to let it upset me and reminded myself of the need to be very specific when booking a room. We said we would like to talk with the manager to explain to him that not only could I not get into the shower because I was unable lift my legs over the bath, but I was barely able to get into the room, that it was too narrow for Wheely. The manager understood and said he would sort the problem out but we needed to wait — perhaps we would like to wait in the bar? So we headed back to the bar for yet another coffee.

My Travels with Wheely

It had taken most of the day, and we were exhausted. Now ensconced in our room, we could finally relax. The room was exquisite. Not only did we have a walk-in shower but a beautiful bath as well. Having been through all the rigmarole of endless cups of coffee, complaining to somebody who clearly was unable to understand us, and finally talking to the manager, I decided a bath was what I wanted. In a way, I felt a little guilty about having made such a fuss. Let's just put it down to a woman's prerogative to change her mind. Perhaps I didn't feel guilty as I reminded myself Wheely was unable to get into the room, and what good was one of us without the other?

I wonder if you can see where this is leading. The temptation to have a bath was so great I was unable to resist it, and between the two of us we attempted to get me in. We clearly hadn't thought this plan through, as rather stupidly we had given no consideration as to how I was going to get out. For the moment, I enjoyed my bath immensely. It was divine to be surrounded by warm water. It had been such a long time since I'd had one that I savoured every moment. Getting out was a little problematic. I was slippery, like a jellied eel, there was nothing to grab on to, and David couldn't help. I now resembled a beached whale. He let the water out of the bath and dried me as much as he was able. This experience wasn't much fun, but with a lot of laughter, we succeeded. Was it worth it? Yes.

The bed was too inviting for us to resist. I wanted to jump straight into it. The sniffles and colds that started on the original plane journey were now coming

Nicky Dalladay

into their own. We were both suffering from the various germs we had acquired, and to cap it all, now we had sore throats. Meanwhile, David was still coughing like a loony and for some unearthly reason I seemed to have contracted conjunctivitis. How did that happen? I'd never had it before. This was so odd. Rarely do we suffer from anything, but by now, on day five, it looked like we were a couple of sickly individuals, which I suppose we really were at this point. With our sensible heads on us we thought there was only one solution: an early night and much-needed sleep.

Day Six
Hanoi, Halong Bay, Hai Phong

Today we left Hanoi and made for Halong Bay (165km east of Hanoi), and as it was a long journey we stopped en route for a break. As if by some miracle, we now found ourselves in some sort of factory outlet with yet another opportunity for us to be sold, this time, the wares of the Vietnamese labour force.

I needed to go to the toilet and found myself trying to fight off five tiny Vietnamese women who were hell-bent on trying to help me all the way. The two of us managed to get into the toilet cubicle, and to be fairly honest I think seven of us would have found it a little bit too cosy. Having successfully gone to the toilet by myself with David, we emerged from the cubicle, only to find that my previous helpers had been outside waiting for me to finish. I am accustomed to David helping me, but I'm not used to having an audience. I shrugged this off and reminded myself that they wanted to help. I was puzzled as to what was going through their minds. Had they not seen a disabled woman before, or was this standard procedure for visitors to their factory?

Now that the toilet situation had been dealt with, I found I was again at the mercy of my five new friends, who whisked me into the factory for a shopping opportunity. Items on sale, all of which were proffered in my direction, consisted of goods ranging from pictures, handbags, and

Nicky Dalladay

silk scarves to everything else you couldn't possibly live without; it reminded me of those funny little books that come with magazines. They were obviously trying to sell us things in order to make a living, but the good thing was that it wasn't done in a hard way. They were smiling and so lovely.

It was terribly cold and there were an awful lot of people working there, ranging from very young to quite elderly — none of whom looked particularly happy or unhappy in their work, just expressionless. They were wearing several layers of clothing, none of which went together, but they didn't seem to care. Fashion clearly had little importance in their lives; it was so far removed from the world I live in. This engulfed me with all sorts of emotions: I felt humble and selfish and realised the futility of the materialistic world. The majority were doing very close embroidery work, which was very skilful and labour intensive. We felt obliged to buy some of their work and did just that. They seemed to want us to buy more and we would have been more than happy to but they just didn't understand we were at the beginning of a long journey.

There were a few smartly dressed people who furnished us with coffee whether we wanted it or not and who rather curiously seemed to want to keep touching me and stroking my hair. Thinking about it, it must have been strange they all had long straight dark hair and were not used to seeing people with brown curly hair.

We clambered into the people carrier to continue our journey to Halong Bay. We were reliably informed by

My Travels with Wheely

Hien, our guide, this is listed as a World Heritage area of outstanding natural beauty, and how right he was. Hien then told us we were about to go on a boat trip and pointed in the general direction. I looked down at the boat and then looked at where we were positioned. I looked down at the boat once more just for clarification and could scarcely believe it. Naturally, it crossed my mind to wonder how on earth we were going to get from A to B without encountering a fatality. The steps down to the boat were just terrifying. They were very narrow and deep. I always wanted to be a stunt woman but realized my wish was going to be granted sooner than I thought. With one eye open and one firmly shut a group of Vietnamese men adeptly lifted me up and carried me down the terrifying steps in Wheely and placed me on a jetty that was hanging on by some good fortune. They continued and carried me down onto the boat because by hook or by crook they were clearly determined I was going to get on.

Once again, I was the recipient of genuine kindness. They reminded me of the special people in Bangkok and the fact that health and safety did not exist in this part of the world, and for that I was eternally grateful. In Halong Bay we experienced the first of our many boat trips in Vietnam. When we got on the large boat, we were somewhat surprised to discover we were the only two passengers; it seemed awfully extravagant to have this boat just for us. They provided us with the most sumptuous feast of prawns, crabs, a beautiful baked fish (identity unknown), spring rolls, rice, and chips — this is where we experienced some of the Western world's influence, great? It was a lovely lunch, and apart from the chips, they really looked after us.

Nicky Dalladay

After lunch, we ventured outside to take in some of the breathtaking views. Apparently, the bay consists of a dense cluster of 1,969 limestone monolithic islands, each topped with thick jungle vegetation that rises spectacularly from the ocean. Several of the islands are hollow with enormous caves. Some support floating villages of fishermen, who ply the shallow waters for two hundred species of fish. Many of the islands have acquired their names as a result of interpretation of their unusual shapes. During the Vietnam War, some of the channels between the islands, heavily mined by the U.S. Navy, pose a threat to shipping to this day. I was intrigued by the floating villages. What must their lives be like, I would never know. I would have liked to have more of an insight but respect their right to privacy. The last thing they want is some tourist poking her nose in. Although it was an overcast day and raining it could not possibly detract from the glorious sights I knew would remain with me forever.

Whilst wending our way back just enjoying the moment, the items for sale appeared once more. We were fast becoming potential shopping targets on our travels but felt slightly guilty that we couldn't possibly purchase every little thing that was proffered in our direction; the donkey train couldn't get larger, unless of course David should turn into the incredible Hulk. There was a beautiful young woman snuggling up to me and stroking my hair, and then she launched into the big sell. Luckily for David he was able to get up and move freely. I had very nearly forgotten what legs were intended for, and without further ado he rose and walked off, leaving me to look at things I really didn't want. *Thanks a bunch*, I quietly thought. Mental note: *I will aim to get him back at some point in the future.*

My Travels with Wheely

The selection of goods on offer at today's shopping extravaganza was anything from an embroidered bag to pictures to jewellery. For a laugh, as there is nothing I like better than to haggle and of course I had been left to fend for myself, I then tried to bargain for something, but she was having none of it. She certainly was a tough cookie, and it was full price or not at all — unfortunately for her — and it was heading toward the latter. In the end, just to appease her, I bought a very small something to get her off my back. She certainly wasn't going to give up that easily and proceeded to get more expensive items out, but alas, that didn't work either. It appeared that neither of us would budge, and that's the way it stayed. She was not on her way to making her first million with me, I'm afraid. Rather amusingly and seemingly content that I wasn't going to make her rich overnight, she produced a rather elderly "learn to speak English" book, and the rest of the journey passed with us trying to understand each other, to no avail.

We arrived back at Halong Bay several hours later, whereby everyone helped me off as gallantly as they had helped me on. The kindness of the Vietnamese, the sights that we saw and the whole experience of the boat trip will remain with me. I am almost certain they will never have any idea of just what they enabled me to do.

Setting off once more we bid a fond farewell to the boat crew to head for Hai Phong. The hotel was nowhere near as nice as the one in Hanoi, but it was decent enough. Naturally, I had reserved a disabled room, and after our first experience in Bangkok assumed that this would not be a problem. Rather strangely and to my amusement, they didn't really get the concept of somebody who was disabled and

Nicky Dalladay

couldn't lift her own body. They somehow thought I could climb into a bath to have a shower. Unbeknownst to us, this problem wasn't going to leave us and would continue for the next three months. The people we had met thus far had been wonderful, accommodating, and extremely helpful. We successfully changed rooms again and spent a pleasant evening in Hai Phong.

E-mail Received

I got your Heathrow e-mail after a little delay at this end. Hope everything is going okay; presumably you survived the long flight to Bangkok. How was the non-smoking? There is nothing much to report at this end. The government is still lashing up everything and the weather is predictable. Take care of yourselves and have a ball. VM.

It was good to know that life at home hadn't really changed in the political arena; mind you, we had only been away for a week. Oops. I had temporarily forgotten about giving up smoking.

Day Seven
Hanoi

We were now roughly a hundred kilometres from Hanoi and had begun to feel like well-seasoned travellers. Hai Phong served as the primary seaport for the northern region of the country. During the war it was subjected to heavy bombing by the United States due to its status as North Vietnam's only major port. After the war, the city was built up as a significant industrial centre. Life in Hai Phong was very busy and colourful. We watched many small women carting fruit and vegetable using a yoke; in fact, this method was used to transport every imaginable thing possible.

The houses there, as they seemed to be in Vietnam, were extremely narrow, and it was very common for the front room at the bottom of the house to be used as a shop. I was awestruck by the way the Vietnamese led their lives. It rather reminded me of expression used by elderly people in the United Kingdom from the days of the Second World War: "make do and mend." The pavements were crumbling, people were squatting beside bins, they were dressed in colourful yet somehow shabby clothing, but the most important thing was that they were smiling.

The day turned into a rather cultural day and was spent by visiting the Opera House, Du Hang pagoda and the Kenh community. We stopped for lunch, which proved a rather odd occasion as I recall — we had no idea what we were eating and thought better of it than to try to ascertain what it was. I had no doubt that if there was anything slightly dubious about it we were sure enough to find out for ourselves later. Fortunately, neither of us is prone to delicate stomachs, the proof being our insides remained intact for the entire day. Lunch was then swiftly followed with a visit to the Ethnology Museum and the Temple of Literature. The cultural experience served as a way to break our long journey back to Hanoi.

In the early evening we attended a performance of the famous Vietnamese traditional art of water puppetry at Thang Long Theatre. Getting into the building was an amazing experience itself, let alone watching the show. The tall thin building had the steepest staircase I'd ever seen in my life, yet all these willing hands rallied forth and lifted me up the stairs. Heads were being banged left, right, and centre but nobody seemed to mind. Hands came from absolutely everywhere to assist in my journey with Wheely to get me into the theatre. Once again, I was nothing but humbled by this unique experience.

The show was so clever and amusing we were in awe of the puppeteers. The only shame was that the musical sound made by the musicians and singers was truly terrible. I don't mean to be rude but it wasn't pleasant and not particularly kind to the ears. The show finally finished and it was time to leave. Of course what goes up must come down. The journey back down the stairs was pretty scary, but they all rallied forth once more and got me down. Our last night in Hanoi was spent in the same hotel as the first night in Vietnam, only this time we didn't encounter any problems with the room, and everything was perfect.

Day Eight
Flight Three, Hanoi to Hue

Hue was the former royal city of the thirteen ruling Nguyen dynasties, so naturally I thought it would be quite a grand place. Upon arrival at Hue you would never know this had once been home to the landed gentry. There were absolutely no facilities to get me down the stairs. Once again I found myself at the mercy of some little Vietnamese men who had to manhandle me down to the tarmac. Only upon arrival at the bottom of the steps it evidently began to dawn on them I would have to have a wheelchair; I could tell from the look on their faces. They frantically began their search for something suitable while I was left dangling in mid air by the ones who were left holding on to me. I was not angry about this — I wasn't even upset — I merely laughed. It seemed such a ludicrous situation to find myself in and definitely one you couldn't plan even if you wanted to.

Having said I was not bothered by this situation, my mind wandered to the league of physiotherapists I have seen in my life. They would certainly not condone this manoeuvre as a good transfer. Well, tough! This was all about getting me from one situation to another. My mind was being somewhat active as the immortal words *drink up* and *brewery* sprang to mind.

Once we had collected all the members of the donkey train, we were met by La^n, which roughly translates to

Nicky Dalladay

a four-legged animal with a single horn on its head. I can only describe him as a somewhat eccentric and very alternative Vietnamese with an American accent. His appearance was very different from the people we had met previously. He had light hair — what little there was of it — and he was quite chunky. He was also a little surprised by Wheely and proceeded to run around like a headless chicken. He was about as helpful as a chocolate teapot. It soon became clear he was more concerned about keeping his ponytail dry as the rain lashed down than he was with helping us. La^n was extremely pleasant albeit rather quirky.

This time they sent a bus as the transport vehicle, which proved quite difficult to ascend, but we somehow managed. Safely on the bus we made our way and visited the Imperial Citadel and Forbidden City. It was quite clear that he had learned his English from an American soldier as he kept using the term "click" when he referred to distance.

We were then taken to our hotel, which on first appearance seemed to fit the bill, and we were shown to our room, which was very nice, but hey presto, it had a bath with a shower in it. We said to the man who took us in that it was a very nice suite but was no good as we really needed a walk-in shower. We made no move to look as though we intended to stay there and waited for the manager. He arrived and showed us to a lovely room with a walk-in shower, proving once more these rooms did exist but you really had to stand your ground.

They really seemed to have no idea of what being

My Travels with Wheely

disabled was about. I firmly believed what I was asking for was quite simple, but it was proving difficult to get my message across. I wasn't so sure this was just a language problem, but I honestly didn't know what it could be. One thing I did know was that it only added to my frustration.

Did life really have to be that difficult? Unfortunately, my life now is full of frustration, I so want to be able to do things when I choose. But I can't, and I still can't accept that I'm disabled. Will I ever?

Day Nine
Hue, Danang, Hoi An

Overnight, it appeared that our guide, La^n, had relinquished all responsibility for us, and a new guide introduced himself as Lanh, meaning quick-minded, smart, and street smart, which sounded good so far. We were picked up from the hotel and taken on a boat trip on the Perfume River to the Thien Mu Pagoda, one of the oldest ancient architectural structures for religious worship in Hue. We continued to visit the Royal tombs of Tu Duc and Khai Dinh. After lunch we started the spectacular drive over Hai Van Pass to Danang and then visited the Cham Museum before continuing to the charming historic city of Hoi An.

Tonight we stayed in a fabulous hotel; the setting was the substance that dreams are made of. The hotel was situated on the most glorious beach I had ever seen. It was just a shame that the weather didn't match up to the beauty. There was a howling gale, the waves came crashing in from the sea, and the palm trees were at right angles to the ground. We certainly didn't let the inclement conditions deter us and set off for a bracing walk along the beach — we are British, after all.

I don't think either of us realized we would see a part of Vietnam that was so unlike the rest. The hustle and bustle of Vietnamese life just didn't exist here; it was almost as if we had entered a time warp. Oddly enough there was nobody on the beach and after being used to the close proximity of

My Travels with Wheely

people, it was kind of strange that we were alone. This was by no means the best day to see this beautiful place, but then better to have seen it this way than not at all.

E-mails Received

One week gone and how has it been? Can't remember where you were going first but I bet is has been lovely. EM

Hope all is going well. L&KO

We heard all about your around-the-world adventure. Whilst we are watching our local MP make an arse of himself on television, you're lapping up the Pacific waves and sunshine, just a bit jealous to say the least. Would you please be so kind as to add us to your mailing list? (I never thought I'd utter those words.) D&S

Hi, Globetrotters. Can't wait to hear more from your next destination although the business class lounge at Heathrow sounds fantastic to us but then, we are but simple country folk now. J&JW

You have only been away for just over a week, so how's it going, is it all amazing? M&JG

We hadn't even been away for a fortnight, but it was nice to read that people were thinking of us.

Day Ten
Hoi An, Danang, HCMC

Today we found we had another boat trip to tackle, but thankfully this went according to plan and without difficulty. It was only a short boat trip across the river to the boat builder's yard, as well as the woodcarvers', pottery, and brick-making village. After that we discovered Hoi An, an ancient town known to early Western merchants as one of the major trading centres of South East Asia in the sixteenth century; with a distinctive Chinese atmosphere, low tiled roof houses, and narrow streets, the original structure of some of the streets was still virtually intact.

Hoi An was a very interesting place, and the architecture was quite beautiful and could only really be appreciated by walking around and getting a feel of the place. We visited a Chinese temple and were once again overwhelmed by the pungent smell of incense. We carried on walking over a tiny bridge and marvelled at how beautiful something could be. Venturing forth into a small museum with a beautiful courtyard, we looked at a replica model of the Great Wall of China; it reminded us of our visit to China many years ago when we witnessed the wall firsthand; such happy memories.

After yet another unknown lunch, our stomachs were certainly holding up very well indeed. We continued our journey, stopping at Marble Mountain. David was invited to climb up the many steps of this amazing mountain to

My Travels with Wheely

view the delights with the guide. On the other hand, I was taken to the marble factory to be shown the delights of what I could buy. The people were very nice and friendly; again they kept touching me and my hair. They insisted on presenting me with copious amounts of tea. I had no wish to be rude so I obliged them by drinking it; this was a true test of how large the capacity of one's bladder could actually be. I knew for a fact that it was more than capable of accommodating a bottle of wine, so a drop of tea shouldn't be too hard.

Much later than I expected David eventually returned and found that I had not bought a large monument for the garden; instead, I was bursting to go to the loo. Must have been something about the amount of tea I drank. An interesting scenario occurred when again we were accompanied by several women to go to the toilet. By this stage I didn't really care who did what. All I knew was I was now desperate for a pee.

We managed to leave the marble shop with the tiniest of purchases. I could see they were disappointed but we had to be strict so as not to acquire too many things because we still had an awful long way to go.

Smiling we watched the lovely views sink into the distance with the happy memories firmly planted in our heads. Just as well really because the weather had been so terrible that I dare say the pictures would not be up to much. Some you win and some you lose.

Lanh bade us farewell and left us at Danang Airport for a transfer to Ho Chi Minh City, or rather Saigon, as

Nicky Dalladay

the locals refer to it.

Flight Four
Danang to Saigon

I could barely believe we were actually in Saigon. In reality I had heard more about Saigon than any other city in Vietnam. Of course the only real introduction was having seen the musical Miss Saigon. I know ... not really similar. For some extraordinary reason we both felt that arriving here was an uplifting experience. Ho Chi Minh — how very different from anywhere else in Vietnam. There was the same hustle and bustle, millions of people on bikes, definitely more money being thrown around, and strange goings on in the hair department. What I mean by that was an awful lot of people went in for highlights. Well, to be more specific, large streaks of bleached blonde stripes on very dark hair. All I can say is: "big mistake"!

We were greeted by a smiling gentleman who introduced himself as Thao, which means courtesy. By now it was quite late in the evening so we were taken straight to our hotel.

We arrived at the hotel but the alien was back, and the spasms in my legs were convulsing like mad and the pain was excruciating. I had what can only be described as a complete sense of humour failure, and I was just annoyed with people man-handling me all the time. They all seemed to want to grab bits of me I didn't want them to grab. I fully realized people were being kind and helpful but everybody seemed to think that by grabbing

My Travels with Wheely

my arms it would be of help. In fact, it was the worst thing anybody could do as my arms were still able to function. I use them to support myself and pull myself up; if they took my arms away I would have nothing, but they didn't know this.

Day Eleven

Up bright and early? Well, Thao wanted to pick us up at 08.00, but they just didn't realize what we had to do in order to get me up, washed, and dressed for the day, so we reached a compromise and eventually settled for 09.00.

We were picked up and were bright and cheerful, which just demonstrates what a good night's sleep can do. Our destination was the Cu Chi province and naturally a stop en route at the obligatory "tat" shop.

We finally arrived at the Cu Chi tunnels, one of the most famous battlegrounds of the Vietnam War. Wow! What an amazingly complex system of underground tunnels. There are more than 200km of tunnels comprising a main axis system and many branches connecting to underground hideouts. The intricacies of the tunnels were purely ingenious. One tunnel entrance is open so that you can go in to experience just what it was like, and David did just that; luckily he's very slim and can get out.

During the war, the Vietnamese people made good use of everything that was merely cast aside and discarded by the Americans. The ammunition boxes were used in the tunnels as toilets and the tyres were made into sandals, so very little was wasted.

On the journey back we visited the post office and

My Travels with Wheely

Presidential Palace; well, strictly speaking it was more of a photo opportunity, really, before being dropped off back at the hotel.

We needed to collect our thoughts the experience of the tunnels was not one to be dismissed

Nicky Dalladay

Cu Chi Tunnels

Day Twelve
Cai Be, Vinh Long, Can Tho

We left Saigon this morning and sat in traffic for about four hours, and there was me thinking the M25 was a dreadful road, but there was no comparison. Eventually, we got to the river where we took a boat trip on the "mighty" Mekong River, following the narrow waterways. The Mekong River is very brown and looked filthy, but amongst all this we saw two small children swimming in the river, laughing out loud, smiling, and waving at us; what a beautiful sight.

Adorning the sides of the river were people's dwellings. I could only describe them as makeshift homes, assembled using pieces of wood and corrugated iron. In amongst all this poverty was an abundance of brightly clothed people, a mass of Vietnamese Cooley hats, and a staggering amount of aerials on every home.

We disembarked the boat to taste yet more delights of heaven only knew what, notwithstanding that they tasted pretty damn good. We were surrounded by vegetation and had entered a construction made from bamboo. It was almost as if it had only been built that morning. This was outdoor dining as we had never experienced before and doubted very much if we ever would again. After lunch, we got on the boat once more and made our way back along the Mekong River, watching the fishermen casting their nets for what I supposed was their next meal.

Nicky Dalladay

On dry land, we clambered back into the vehicle and made our way to the war museum. You would surely have a heart of stone not to be affected by the harrowing pictures we saw. The museum was first opened to the public in 1975, its primary role being to collect, preserve, and display exhibits on war crimes. One of the key displays is the issue of Agent Orange. We saw images of how the toxin actually affects living people and unborn foetuses in various unpleasant ways, and numerous photos showing humans born with deformations due to their families living in areas that were sprayed.

Never having experienced any sort of war before, let alone this one, I was deeply moved by the photographs.

We were dropped off in Can Tho at our next hotel, which was so extreme from everything we had witnessed today. I was reminded just how privileged I am to live in the society I do. It would be wrong for us to interfere and try and change this country to suit us, but you can see that it's necessary to enhance the infrastructure whilst preserving the very essence of the people who live here. Whilst we were surrounded by abject poverty, we had yet to see anyone who looked unhappy. I was also very aware just how much a country like this needs tourism, but couldn't help but think that at sometime in the future the tourists of tomorrow will be responsible for ruining what there was at the moment.

We arrived in our room, which was gorgeous, and absolutely everything was perfect. It had been a hot and sticky day so I decided to take my rings off and soak them in the basin, which proved not to be a good move. Whilst

My Travels with Wheely

taking them out I slid them up the side of the sink but had failed to notice that there was a small hole and they both fell into it.

As I didn't know what else to do I called housekeeping to see if they could help. Within minutes a pleasant young man was dispatched to our room to try and retrieve them. He practically dismantled the sink, and the bathroom now resembled the Mekong, but he actually found them; what a brilliant man.

Mental note: *Take notice in future of small holes in sinks.*

Day Thirteen

Today was Tet (lunar New Year), and for this reason there were no organized trips. The guide and driver were nowhere near their families, so they very kindly offered to take us out. They picked us up, and we walked into downtown Can Tho, which boasted an incredible flower market. They were so kind, and Thao our guide took over and pushed me everywhere. He was quite good at negotiating the badly cracked pavements. It was so hot he insisted I purchase a hat and promptly stopped in the market where they were actually hand making traditional conical Vietnamese hats. He was even going to pay for it, but we managed to get there first and paid the princely sum of $1.00. I suppose I looked pretty silly, but it did the job of keeping the sun off.

We had such a lovely day with them, and they showed us as much as they could. On making our way back to the hotel, an old man on an equally old bicycle was wearing the traditional hat turned around and did a double take. My guess was he was not that familiar with seeing a "bird" in a wheelchair wearing the Vietnamese hat. He kept turning to look at me. I really believed he was wobbling so much that he might fall off his bike, at which point I smiled at him and he smiled back, revealing a lovely smile and showing me his one tooth. To think of it, lots of people had been looking at us rather curiously, but as soon as you smiled at them they returned it.

My Travels with Wheely

As a thank you we invited the guide and driver in to have a drink with us. When they left us and returned to where they were staying I couldn't help but wonder what their accommodations were like. I felt sure they would be nothing like ours.

Day Fourteen

We got up early, and it was really early for us to telephone home. We knew our closest friends were having dinner to celebrate a birthday, and we called them. We had only been away for a couple of weeks, but because we had achieved so much, it felt longer. They were pleased to hear from us, and we promptly got passed around the table, visualizing where each of them was sitting. They were very boisterous and somewhat intoxicated, and it was so lovely talking to them all.

We encountered another long drive today, stopping at Soc Trang for a final temple visit. The temple was just heaving with people, and more importantly, everybody seemed to be holding at least forty Joss sticks each. I am a person who is surrounded by clouds of smoke every day of my life but this was incredible; you could barely see your hands in front of you. It resembled a thoroughfare and was nothing like any religious service I had ever been to before. Everybody was just milling around making noises and rocking back and forth.

In order to escape the smoke-filled temple, we went outside for some fresh air. There were as many people outside as there were in, but suddenly I become conscious that four little people were looking at me, smiling. I gestured to who I believed was their mother to ask if I could take a photograph of them, uncertain of her answer but sure she didn't seem to mind David

My Travels with Wheely

taking some photographs. We showed the children and their mother what we had taken, and they giggled with delight but looked slightly bewildered to see their images on the camera.

We got back into the car for the last time as our final destination in Vietnam would be our hotel in Ho Chi Minh.

E-mail Received

You must be well into your tour by now and will have sampled the delights and chaos that is Bangkok! You have such a long trip; the beginning will be a distant memory by the time you get to the end. Enjoy every moment and think of us all in the cold every now and then. WR

How right she was! We had sampled chaos unlike we had ever experienced before, and it was just a fantastic.

Day Fifteen
Flight Five, Saigon to Singapore

Today we left Vietnam's Tan Son Nhat International Airport on our flight to Singapore before flying to Perth, Australia. On our way to the airport we passed through Chinatown, and although it was their New Year today there was as much hustle and bustle as ever, with maybe one or two fewer bikes. We also saw our first rat today, which was utterly amazing when you considered the filth around you; I was just surprised I hadn't seen a lot more of them.

In Vietnam there was such an eclectic mix of things: extreme poverty, and tremendous filth and grime everywhere you looked. They lived in conditions quite unknown to us yet they all seemed happy, and the people were so wonderfully kind. They were amazingly clean and dressed their children as well as themselves beautifully. They were certainly not followers of fashion in any way and you might be so bold to say that there was a fashion faux pas going on wherever you turned, but they just didn't seem to care and neither should they.

This had been a unique experience in such a beautiful country with a very friendly and handsomely petite race of people who have yet to be ruined by the West, although the Western influence has well and truly arrived in Ho Chi Minh with the arrival of all the fast food chains, and as a result, larger people. We are indeed fortunate people

My Travels with Wheely

to have been given such insight to a fabulous country and terrific people.

We were lucky enough to realize our dreams, embrace new cultures, and discover cuisine like we had never tasted before or since. There was an awful lot to laugh about, and we certainly had fun. There were, of course, the frustrations that we both encountered. Vietnam was clearly not a place designed for the disabled yet, and I made sure that I factored this in at the time of booking. At the outset, I had been warned I wouldn't be able to participate in some things but of course David could. On the trips I couldn't possibly contemplate he took lots of pictures to show me of things I was unable to see.

Second E-mail
From Transit Singapore Business Lounge

The e-mail that I sent from Singapore was recapping our experiences that have already been written about. Replies that follow relate to that text. I have no wish to slow the story down so have removed the bulk of the message.

...As you can see we passed through Heathrow with relative ease, ready to embark on our 'round-the-world trip lasting just over three months. Our next stop is Perth, and we arrive in the early hours tomorrow. Not sure when our next communication will be as the internal flights in Australia will only be economy. Thought we'd slum it!

Love to everyone
The DallAwayDays
xxxx

Nicky Dalladay

There was oodles of time to while away on the Internet; how I loved the facilities. There was certainly enough spare time to read several messages.

E-mails Received

Wonderful travelogue and a useful bit of information that one would need to lose three stone before visiting Thailand! Presumably that's why they use elephants so much for transport; it's the only thing the tourists can fit on. EA

On a dreary Monday morning, when the atmosphere in the office is even more depressing than the weather, it is thoroughly refreshing to read about your travels and experiences. I'm really chuffed for you both and pleased you're both enjoying it so much. CB

Wow! So far it all sounds as though it's absolutely fantastic despite your both having colds and sore throats. So glad that the people you've met so far have been smashing from the sound of it. I can quite understand how you must feel confronted by the tiniest people on Earth; we must all seem like elephants in comparison! M&JG

Fantastic reading, thank you, take care, I very much look forward to the next missive. AA

I hope it will it be all right if I include some of your adventures in the next Pensioners' Newsletter? Have a great time in Australia. RC

It is so good to hear from you, and what an amazing

My Travels with Wheely

experience you're having. Promise I won't rabbit on too much, because by the sound of things, you don't have much time to touch sides. Hope the rash on your legs is better, Nicky, and your cold over by now, David. NB

It's absolutely fabulous to get all of your news. It's all amazing whether positive or not quite so. LE

Hi, it's great to hear from you and of course to hear about your impressions and experiences. I thought I could time a response to fit in with Singapore Airport. Weather very cold here at the moment … work grinds on … just the sort of thing I expect you like to hear! GD

It was wonderful to have messages from home, we were glad they wanted to hear from us, and nice to know the oldies would get to read about our travels.

Day Sixteen
Flight Six, Singapore to Australia

I was very pleased to report that no aliens visited me during the flight; I might even go as far as to say it was quite comfortable. We were on the next leg of our journey and couldn't quite believe we were about to touch down on Australian soil. The excitement that we felt was a magical feeling, and I imagined it was one that would be hard to replace with anything.

We arrived in Perth in the early hours of the morning and our first impressions of the people were what a miserable bunch of sods they were. Oh dear, we were not off to a very good start. The airport was very strict and all items of baggage were x-rayed when entering the country. They were so exacting that they confiscated a chocolate bar that had not even been opened yet and therefore not touched by human hands. It almost felt like we were convicts trying to enter their precious country. I seemed to recall that their country was based on the arrival of convicts initially, but it just showed how times had changed. They now had the audacity to be picky.

After some hours, they eventually granted us permission and had decided it was perfectly legitimate to enter their country, so we left the airport to search for a taxi. We managed to pick up a taxi to take us on the half hour journey to Scarborough, where we were staying. Even though we were both tired, we were still very excited and

My Travels with Wheely

really wanted to engage in conversation with our new friend, the taxi driver. To our amazement he was having none of it; he didn't utter a single word, he just snorted and grunted; his name must surely be "Mr. Snort." I would say that by now Mr. Snort's chances of receiving any tip from us were diminishing by the minute.

Our first impressions of Perth were of the enormous roads and just how deserted they were; mind you it was the early hours of the morning. We were by now in the suburbs of Perth, but we could have been just about anywhere.

Miserable Mr. Snort suddenly had a personality transformation and decided that now he was going to be helpful. Call me a cynic but I believe he was merely after a decent tip, but I'm afraid it was a case of too little, too late.

The donkey train made its way into the hotel, and we were greeted by a night watchman who confirmed our reservation and relieved us of one of our many vouchers, punched a few things into his keyboard, and confirmed that we had been booked into a "handicapped room." He then watched David assemble the donkey train. He picked up a set of keys, yawned, and then showed us to our room.

The stop in Scarborough was planned and had intended to be a rest period, so with that in mind, we had been quite specific about our requirements, knowing full well we would be spending a good few days here. We had gone to the trouble of booking an ocean view room, with romantic notions of sitting on the balcony sipping our gin and tonic, breathing the fresh sea air, and just taking in the gorgeous view.

This was an example of how the best laid plans could go horribly wrong. Our view was not looking at the ocean. We were, in fact, overlooking a petrol station, fast food outlets and shops, which was all well and good if you had a penchant for looking at petrol stations. To be fair, you could see the ocean — if you were a contortionist and craned your neck to the right much further than it was designed to go — you could actually see it. Strictly speaking, David could do all of the above, which demonstrated height and agility was, a distinct advantage, but I couldn't.

Now we turned our attention to the room which was as promised a disabled room, or rather handicapped room, with all the right ingredients. Well, a walk-in shower. However, there was something quite awful about the room. It smelt musty and horrible, like nobody had slept there for a year or so. In fact, I wouldn't have been at all surprised to come across a corpse covered in cobwebs. By now it was very late, or early depending on which way you looked at it, and we were so tired we needed some sleep desperately. "Tomorrow is another day," and we would tackle our disillusionment in the morning.

E-mails Received

Quite an experience you're having, although it doesn't all sound totally comfortable. I guess that's inevitable! I should think you will see quite a contrast now that

My Travels with Wheely

you are in Oz. We went up to Chinatown on Sunday for their New Year, and the only problem is there were loudspeakers all around with KL welcoming everyone … am going to reread Orwell's 1984: it's becoming a reality. VM

It sounds like a fantastic experience so far. I think you will find Perth less polluted. JS

Interesting to learn what went on in London for Chinese New Year. I had a feeling it was very different from Tet in Vietnam.

Day Seventeen
Scarborough

With recharged batteries and feeling much fresher after a night's sleep, we made our way to the reception to talk to the manager. With great ease we managed to get our room changed to a proper ocean view room; we could both see the view now. It was a spectacular day and the sun shined; we were much happier. I doubted very much we would miss the view of the petrol station. I shall never cease to be amazed at what people are prepared to palm you off with. The room smelt much cleaner and fresher; this was the type of room we had originally anticipated.

The first one they had put us in, the disabled room, rather made you feel that; because you were less than able you had lost all sense of taste and had no feelings whatsoever. I just didn't get it. Yes I am disabled, but I am still a person who is proud and most certainly has feelings. Why do I continually find I am treated this way? I was rather inclined to think that you should just put up and shut up, and I was angered feeling this way; it was not right. They had picked the wrong girl to mess with.

The hotel rather resembled something from the Eastern Block of around forty years ago. The corridors were very long, and I almost expected to see a large woman wearing a grey dress sitting at the end of the hallway, whose job it was to monitor all the comings and goings of the inmates. It was very strange.

My Travels with Wheely

We went for a long stroll by the beach, and by god it was windy but very hot. It was the most glorious day and wonderful to take in the fresh sea air. We hadn't even been here for a day yet and it was then it occurred to me we had left the land of the slim beautiful people and had arrived in the fat, ugly gits land, where I now felt positively thin.

I sat on the balcony, having a cigarette — oops, I've done it again — never mind, there's always Sydney. It was early in the evening and David had located the guest laundry area. After two weeks of travelling we had managed to amass a mountain of dirty clothes. In Australia, it was quite normal for the hotels to have laundry facilities rather like a launderette. He gathered together the clothes and disappeared to mingle with the natives to do our washing. When he got there he found he was not alone; a couple of elderly American ladies were dab hands at this kind of thing and guided him through the joys of doing your laundry in a hotel. What a novel experience.

He arrived back a couple of hours later, and at 21.00 we strolled out of the hotel to see what fine dining experiences in the area were on offer, or perhaps I should say more accurately, that was the plan. We set off, but Scarborough seemed suspiciously closed. Our fears were confirmed when we entered a few restaurants and were told they were no longer serving. Finally, at the last restaurant, we tentatively went in, only to find they were starting to put the chairs on the table. It looked as though we were not going to be eating tonight. Someone took pity on us; I would like to think it was because we

Nicky Dalladay

looked so emaciated in comparison to everybody else and obviously needed feeding. We were told that we were quite welcome to have coffee and a cake, just as long as we were quick.

We were warned, and somebody hovered over us to take an order. Within minutes, David was served a slab of carrot cake and I had a chocolate muffin served with butter. I still remain puzzled as to why it was accompanied by butter. For fear of outstaying our welcome, David wolfed his cake down while I shovelled mine around the plate; it was disgusting, but in that respect, good for the diet. They didn't seem to complete their service there as you had to go up to someone to ask for the bill and pay there and then, which was very odd. Come to think of it, what service? They proceeded to continue with putting the chairs on the tables whilst people finished their meals; perhaps they didn't want us there.

It seemed to me that this destination was a bit of a hole with no life whatsoever, although this was apparently peak season. I would hate to be there when it was quiet. Oh dear, I am acutely aware that I was beginning to sound like a "whinging pom." I really don't want to sound like that, but sometimes in life the most memorable things are often the worst.

With the benefit of hindsight we should not have made Perth our first destination in Australia, as we were in a suburb and didn't really get a feel for the city itself. In fact, I didn't warm to the Australians in Scarborough. As far as I was concerned they were perfect twats. One guy dropped a door in our faces; I was almost certain he saw

My Travels with Wheely

us coming but couldn't be bothered to wait a few more seconds. Another person had parked over the disabled ramp at the hotel and David had to lift Wheely and me up the steps. For the umpteenth time, my heart went out to him. He could really do without this inconvenience, particularly when there were the facilities in place but you just couldn't use them. People just don't think, and that was rather upsetting. I was really unimpressed with this place so far and could only hope it would get better tomorrow.

Day Eighteen

Indeed it did get better. Today we ventured to Hillary's Boat Harbour, which took about forty-five minutes' walk to get to. Interestingly enough, they maintained that there was so much to do there that it was quite likely you would arrive for breakfast and end up staying for days. Apparently, this all-season resort offered entertainment, first class shopping, leisure, and fine dining. Mm, I think their marketing team was perhaps a little overzealous with their narrative.

We went to the aquarium and took the underwater journey to discover the incredible unique marine life of Western Australia. The more adventurous amongst us were invited to snorkel or dive with the sharks, and in spite of my encouragement, David declined, which rather surprised me. When I said us, I meant David, Wheely, and me, as other people weren't evident.

Under their fine-dining section we read there were nineteen restaurants available, although it has to be said that we did in fact struggle to find them. If nothing else, we were very persistent, and by walking further afield our efforts paid off; we found a gorgeous restaurant and sat outside just gazing at the wonderful yachts. And do you know what? I might surprise you now by saying we had a lovely lunch.

It was the most beautiful, serene place, but sadly a

My Travels with Wheely

little spoilt by the naff eateries and seriously obese folk shovelling all they could down their necks. It really went against what we thought the Australians would be like, all slim, fit, and sporty. Of course our knowledge was really based on films we had seen — hardly reality was it? We did have a lovely relaxing day and were just happy to stroll around.

To be forewarned is to be forearmed, and with our dining-out experience on the previous evening we decided not to make the same mistake again. We found ourselves getting ready to go out for dinner really early, 18.30 in fact, which is not a time we are accustomed to going out in the evening, but as they say, when in Rome.

We found a nice-looking restaurant and sat outside in the warmth of the evening. A waitress then appeared as if from nowhere, gave us a menu, and took David's order for two gin and tonics. We were a little taken aback when we were told, quite politely, it was illegal here in Scarborough to have a drink without eating. We asked if we could perhaps have a drink whilst contemplating the menu, but the answer was no. Dinner was quite a rushed affair. There was a little break between courses, and just when you swallowed your last mouthful, you were presented with the bill.

We started to make our way back to the hotel when there was a dramatic change in the weather; it was now so windy that if I could stand I would have been blown over. At least David had Wheely to hold onto. I had never known such windy conditions before. Bear in mind the restaurant was very close in the first place and

Nicky Dalladay

the strength of the wind prohibited us from making a fast journey, but we were still back in our hotel room by 20.30. We concluded that going out for dinner here proved that your body was merely a vessel made just to receive food.

For us, this evening was jolly strange, as to go out to dinner is usually for the enjoyment and experience of doing just that. It was certainly not something to be hurried, and we just didn't do the rushing thing. At the outset, I did say we looked forward to experiencing new cultures, and in all fairness this was one of them.

Day Nineteen

Today, we decided to go a bit further afield and went to Caversham Wildlife Park, which entailed a thirty-minute taxi ride at a cost of fifty bucks. It was boiling hot, with amazing blue skies, and to our great relief we had moved away from the terrific winds of Scarborough. The park covered an enormous area and was beautifully presented. We were introduced to kangaroos, wombats, dingos, lorikeets, wallaby, and plenty more animals and birds, some of which we had never heard of before.

We duly noted they offered camel riding. I seriously considered this, but alas, the sensible side of me prevailed. It would have been quite hopeless and impossible. How did I expect Wheely and I to get up on to a camel? I decided that perhaps this was not one of my better ideas and would give this a wide berth for now.

Back to what we were able to do — in some of the enclosures, you could walk around quite freely; you could say we were at one with nature.

We arrived back at the hotel from a lovely day out. Oddly enough, neither of us was particularly hungry and realized our appetites in general had shrunk. I could only assume this was because it was so hot.

I asked David to get me onto the balcony for a cigarette; yes I am still smoking, as previously mentioned, although it was becoming increasingly difficult as Australia

Nicky Dalladay

appeared to have a smoking ban just about everywhere. It was blowing an absolute howler and the ash came from my cigarette faster than I could smoke it. That's one way of cutting down.

Scarborough at this time of the year was not the place to visit for those that are remotely concerned about their coiffure hairstyle; I could categorically say that no amount of hair product would keep your hair in place.

Day Twenty

Still blistering hot, we decided to take advantage of the fact that there was a swimming pool located on the tenth floor of the hotel, so to give David a rest from pushing me around we spent the day there. We were sat there enjoying the heat when a lady started talking to me and introduced herself as Pauline and her husband, Ian. They immigrated to Oz eighteen years ago, and it transpired that three of her sisters had done the same and her parents were on the verge of it. The reason that they were at the hotel was to celebrate their wedding anniversary; they were so in love it was beautiful to see.

Pauline was very keen that I got into the pool; I tried to explain it was not something I could physically do. The fact that I didn't even have a swimming costume on was not enough to deter her from her mission; she was having none of it. By hook or by crook I was getting in, and with her and David's help we got me in. I can't tell you how wonderful it was to be in the water. Unable to swim anymore I just sat in the pool and enjoyed, and I was very grateful to her. This was an example of a very kind person who had popped into my life briefly; almost certainly, I would never see her again.

David did a little bit more housekeeping today and visited the laundry again just to set us up for going to Sydney. It was quite interesting how one could fall into a role so quickly, almost like a gender reversal. He seemed

Nicky Dalladay

to be keen on doing his washing, and I was getting the distinct impression that he was enjoying the company of the "Widow Twankys" in the laundry room.

On his return, he set me straight; he was just getting organized for our impending flight to Sydney, which was very commendable, and anyway, he said, "I have just met some new people." Whilst he was doing his chores in the laundry room, this time David told me he had now met "Ms. & Ms. Golightly." He rather thought they were going to launch into conversation, but in fact there was but one topic they were interested in, and that was food. They made him feel as though he was the representative for the good food guide of Scarborough. Which restaurants had he been to, and were the portions a good, healthy size? In other words, were they large? From the little he had told me about the Ms. & Ms. Golightly, I had already imagined what they must look like. We saw them later that evening, having obviously successfully foraged for food and wearing the dress code of the slightly larger person: an oversized T-shirt and leggings.

I was puzzled by why anyone should want to move to Perth — or more specifically, Scarborough. We had met quite a few nice people, a few pleasant Australians, and the rest tended to be English, but most of the people we met were just plain rude. This was obviously a sweeping statement as we had only touched on a tiny part of Perth, and to be fair we didn't know what the rest was like. I really hoped that the service, or rather lack of it, was not indicative of Australia as a whole. It remained to be seen.

Day Twenty-one
Flight Seven, Perth to Sydney

We left Perth at 09.00 and arrived in Sydney at 16.00. It was a four-hour flight with a three-hour time difference. As we approached we saw the Sydney Opera House and were surprised at how small it looked. I guessed that would change when we stood next to it. We pinched ourselves, and I squealed with delight. We couldn't quite believe we were here.

We checked into the hotel, and amazingly enough we had a room with a walk-in shower and an interesting view of something like spaghetti junction. Other than that, it was a somewhat uneventful day, as it had taken the whole day to get here. Having travelled all day you'd expect to be tired but we weren't, and we headed straight for the nearest bar for a beer — well, wine for me — and a smoked salmon bagel. We were encouraged that at least here you were allowed to have a drink without having to eat.

Back at the hotel it dawned on us that on this leg of our journey we really only had one full day in Sydney, so we would need to make an effort to get up early.

Day Twenty-two

It was now more than three weeks since we had left home, and it seemed to us as though it had been an awful lot longer. So far we had been on seven aeroplane journeys and stayed in several hotels, but our computer case that contained all of our travel documents had not seemed to have reduced much.

In order to make the most of our day we had set our alarm for 07.00 but didn't hear it until 08.00. It was the most pathetic noise you have ever heard, one that resembled an ailing mosquito. Oh well, we got up after "squatting" the alarm and set off much later than anticipated.

We walked in the direction of the Sydney Opera House, and en route popped into Tiffany's (not for the last time) to get a ball that had fallen off David's key ring. What a result, for David we had just been into Tiffany's and had not purchased a single thing. Please bear in mind I did vow to get him back earlier when we were in Vietnam. It will only be a matter of time before I do just that. As well as looking like an elephant I have the memory of one as well, particularly where shopping is concerned.

The opera house was amazing, but rather unfortunately, I was unable to gain access into it as they were undergoing a lot of renovation work, so wheelchairs were strictly verboten. However, we managed to walk all the way

My Travels with Wheely

around it and take lots of pictures. We stopped to have a drink and visited the opera house shop so that I could purchase my memorabilia; much to David's horror, I wanted to buy a mini opera house, and for the life of me I couldn't see why he was so opposed to this.

Whilst we were travelling light I felt it was still important to pick up small pieces so that when we eventually got home we would be reminded of some of the places we had been fortunate enough to visit. Mental note: *don't take any notice of David telling me not to buy the small pieces, I know he'll regret it if I don't.*

We continued our walk around the harbour on what was another scorching day. It was beautiful and certainly the best way to see Sydney in brilliant sunshine. We decided to take a boat trip, which proved to be another bad hair day as it was so windy; obviously it would be, since we were on a boat. The trip was so lovely it was just such a shame you couldn't hear the commentary. The wind was so great it precluded us from hearing. In addition, there were about twenty-four million (never one to exaggerate) Japanese tourists clicking away on their cameras. Incidentally, I featured quite a lot in their photos as they only seemed to take them of each other, and include anyone nearby. They were totally dismissive of the magnificent scenery. How very odd was that?

What next? A visit to the sky tower was a must to see the land that we surveyed. The tower happens to be conveniently situated in the heart of the city, and it takes you to the highest point of Sydney for breathtaking 360° views of beautiful harbour sights. It soars 250m

Nicky Dalladay

above the city streets; the observation deck was reputedly the highest in the Southern hemisphere and offered a panoramic viewing experience. It certainly did what the book said it would do, and it was absolutely spectacular.

Several photographs later, we found ourselves walking through Hyde Park. It struck us as strange just how many names of places are duplicated around the world. It was home to the very beautiful Royal Botanical Gardens, but the layout was completely useless for Wheely, as there were so many steps, resulting in David having to push me back over our tracks so we could walk along the pavement.

Reading the visitor information map we noted with interest the things you were allowed to do and those you weren't. We were invited to smell the flowers, hug the trees (which in my mind seemed just a little odd), picnic on the lawn, and believe it or not, in this squeaky-clean society, walk on the grass. The foliage was so enormous in the botanical gardens, I had never seen anything quite like it before; the plants, most of which I didn't even recognise, were beautiful.

We then crossed the road into Liverpool Street; it seemed a little peculiar because as we know, it's nowhere near Hyde Park. As luck would have it we stumbled upon a branch of Starbucks and decided that it was high time for a cappuccino and muffin. I believe I mentioned earlier the loss of appetite; it seemed they have staged a comeback.

From the opera house we walked to Darling Harbour,

My Travels with Wheely

where our hotel was situated, and what a treat, it was a gorgeous setting. We selected a restaurant and had a beautiful dinner that night, probably our second proper dinner of the trip.

E-mail Received

Vietnam sounds amazing. Can't wait to hear all the details and see the pictures. Keep a note of best things you did for me, would appreciate top tips when I finally get going. Enjoy every minute of your trip. EB

I liked this and it made me think perhaps I could become a travel consultant for the disabled when I got home. After three weeks I already felt over qualified for that particular role.

Day Twenty-three

Today we were picked up from our hotel to go on our trip to the Blue Mountains. The chap picking us up was somewhat surprised that I was in a wheelchair and promptly asked, "Are you able to walk?" I found myself having to bite my tongue. What a stupid question. I really wanted to retort that I enjoyed sitting on my fat arse just for the hell of it, but needless to say, I just said I couldn't. The reason for carefully planning out our trip of this enormity in the first place was to eliminate any possible confusion or disappointments. He had the audacity to be a little put out by Wheely and me, as if I had asked to be disabled in the first place. I was instantly made to feel that I was a great inconvenience; this is something I have to battle with practically every day of my life. He made a telephone call to his boss. I'm not entirely sure why he did this, probably to bleat on about the fact that he had been confronted with a disabled bird and to ask for a different bus. In this day and age I was amazed at his reaction. How dare he make me feel like this?

Anyway, he couldn't alter the bus, and we had to make do with what was available and that was that. Much manhandling then ensued, and the occupants of the coach just gawped at me as if I was a freak show. I was, at last, finally on board. He then informed me he was a paramedic. Not quite sure why he felt the need to share this information with me, but at least he got it off his chest, and oh, his name was Max. Obviously, the

My Travels with Wheely

trip didn't get off to a very good start, but it certainly improved. The tour was amazing, seeing a lot of animals in their natural environment, although it suffered from some lousy misty, grey, miserable weather, which was just bad luck.

Nobody had forced me to go on a journey around the world; it was something I had wanted to do. I felt very much that because I am disabled, for some unearthly reason I had a responsibility for representing people who are in wheelchairs and had to keep smiling so as not to give us a bad name. That statement is utterly ridiculous. I'm a human being who loves to travel whether I'm intrinsically nice or not. The truth is, there are many times when I have to wear my "everything's all right" face no matter how I feel to make it more comfortable for those around me.

Max actually turned a corner in his communication skills, and turned out to be a super chap. In the end he gave me a lot of assistance. I still think he acted inappropriately at the beginning of our tour, and I would just put that down to lack of experience. One thing he said that made me chuckle was, "I'll bet you were a real looker in your day." I quite understood why Australian men got the reputation they did; they earned it. What a cheek, he tactfully avoided my question about what age he thought I was. It merely left me shuddering and checking out my "laughter lines" in the mirror.

At one point he really pulled out all the stops; there was a view everyone went to see but there was no way Wheely and me could get there. He didn't want me to miss out

Nicky Dalladay

on it so he and David carried me down by linking their arms together. Max took a picture of us both and it is the only one of me standing clinging on to David for dear life, and it was a truly special moment.

We were then deposited at the most beautiful hotel, Lilianfels. It was very plush, and we felt it was way too smart for us travelling folk. It was a lovely setting, but there was nothing to do around these parts so I spent an hour on the Internet composing my next e-mail. My time was now up, and David, Wheely, and I went in search of the shop. We had trouble locating anything that resembled a shop until we stumbled across something we thought might fit the bill. Cautiously we entered what was a very large room containing a few shelves with next to nothing on them, and made our way to the counter and asked the man behind if he happened to sell cigarettes. He begrudgingly informed us he did. One wondered why he bothered to sell them. David purchased a packet for me and we left.

David, Wheely, and the "puffing Billy," yours truly, made our way back to the hotel. We were there until lunchtime tomorrow, and as we didn't have any specific plans we were not sure how we were going to fill our time. Ah, then we struck gold. Well, nearly. In the afternoon they served a good old-fashioned full cream tea; it was too much to resist and we indulged ourselves. *This should keep us occupied for a while*, we thought. It was very peaceful here and we just spent the rest of the day chilling.

My Travels with Wheely

Third E-mail

Where were we, ah yes, I remember Singapore Airport's departure lounge. We arrived in Perth late at night and were shown to the "handicapped room." It would seem that being disabled; you have lost the right to your feelings and any possible taste! Anyway, next morning got the room sorted out and got a much better one with an ocean view instead of the petrol station and a shopping centre.

Now we are here for six days; let's see what we can find. We are at Scarborough beach, which is beautiful, apparently one of the best in Australia but by god is it windy, if I could stand I'd certainly be blown over.

Oh my god, first discovery that we have well and truly left the land of the beautiful, thin people of Asia and are deeply immersed in the land of the larger-build, unattractive, homo sapiens, with McDonalds and KFC being the dish of the day.

It was intended that this was to be a rest period after a hectic time in Vietnam. Just as well really because there isn't much to do around these parts except eat and eat again. Talking of eating, that was an interesting experience, on our first night we went out for dinner; or rather we thought we were going out for dinner, only to find that Scarborough appeared to be shut at 21.00. Mm, well, dinner was clearly off the menu. No alcoholic beverages were available, because guess what? In good old Scarborough, you are unable to buy a drink without eating unless in a pub. Over the course of the following

Nicky Dalladay

five days, that went down really well (not), with Mr. D, the poor bloke, who deserved at least an afternoon beer after all the pushing around he's been doing.

We managed to get to a few interesting places, like Cavendish Wildlife Park where David nearly traded me in for a wombat because they were sweet and furry. I shudder to think why he would want to do that.

We left Perth to venture forth to Sydney and the re-introduction of the slim, fit, and good-looking people. Here we felt more at home. We found Sydney an awesome experience just how you'd expect it to be, vibrant and cosmopolitan. We only really had one full day but we tried to make the best of it, well nearly. David set the alarm for 07.00 and at nearly 08.00 we woke up to a pathetic noise from the alarm clock, won't be doing that again. Undaunted by the lousy start the intrepid explorers were off, on foot of course, again to do Sydney in one day. Up the sky tower and its fantastic 360° views, on to the opera house via Tiffany (another branch I can knock off my list). *What did she buy?* I hear you cry. Alas, nothing. Right, now at the Sydney Opera House, how do we get in? Ah, a bit of a problem; you don't. But not to be put off by this we decide it's probably not worth bothering with anyway and proceeded to photograph it from many different points.

Just to digress for a moment, that reminds me: we shall be booking viewing times (or rather days) when we get home, we've taken around five hundred photos to date. I'll bet you're all very busy for the next year now I've mentioned that one.

My Travels with Wheely

I regret that our hour is nearly up on the internet and have to send our message. Will finish off on Sydney next chance we get.

Thanks to those who have sent us e-mails; it really is much appreciated.

Love to everyone
DallAwayDays
xxxx

Nicky Dalladay

Clinging on in The Blue Mountains

Day Twenty-four

Awoke to glorious blue skies once again, and we hot footed it to retake some of yesterday's pictures, but this time in the glorious sunshine. How different it looked today. With the sun shining brightly you could now fully appreciate the stunning beauty of the Blue Mountains, and all of the views were magnificent, as was the sight of the three sisters, the famous rock formation.

We were picked up from the hotel and taken to Featherdale Wildlife Park on our way back to Sydney. It was a very nice park but a little bit confusing when you got in there. They had a fantastic array of birds, many of which had fabulous colourings. We were introduced to a koala bear and had the obligatory photographs taken with it whilst he or she was asleep.

Safely back on the bus I was comforted by reading the conditions on the entry ticket once I had departed the park. Where I read the warnings that "animals can be dangerous and can cause injury" and that my viewing is "on the condition you exercise care and common sense" and that Featherdale would "not be liable" for my death, I was glad I had been nice to David as I could have quite easily ended up residing in the reptile house.

We arrived back in Sydney where we were due to spend the next two nights; bit of a bonus that we got an extra day because we had misread the itinerary. So

Nicky Dalladay

we ventured out to Darling Harbour, where we spent an hour or so dithering about where we should go to eat. Spoilt for choice and with no curfew on time of eating, it was a tricky decision.

Sometime later the same evening we eventually settled on Jordan's Fish Restaurant. I chose the low fat option of Jordan's world famous deep fried fish and chips, whilst David went for the local fish, a barramundi, and a salad. I hated him; he always made such a healthy choice, whereas I on the other hand am prone to making bad decisions. Perhaps that's why he's so slim and I'm on the chubby side. By the way, my choice was made because it was the one and only "world famous Jordan's." I enquired as to what made it world famous and was told, with some pride, it was because they had been in business for ten years. Now forgive me, but I felt that was a little limp, thus in my mind proving that Australians have no class.

Back at our hotel we decided to go for a swift beer. Well, you know what I really mean — I am not a beer drinker, I just happen to like the expression. In the bar we met three people who had been on the Blue Mountain trip and joined them for a drink: Dawn, aged sixty-seven, her sister, Christine, fifty-seven, with her husband, Roy, age not divulged. They were a really nice group of people I think from Manchester, Grimsby. Unlikely our paths would ever cross again as they were due to go home very soon having been travelling for six weeks. It was nice to have met them. Dawn had lost her husband a few years ago, so it was obviously a hard trip for her to make, but good on her for doing it.

My Travels with Wheely

E-mail Received

I do hope you had a wonderful time during your visit to Lilianfels Blue Mountains Resort. When planning your next getaway, and would like to experience the signature luxury, comfort, and personalized service of the Orient Express Trains, please consider our sister property....

We'll remember this e-mail when we get to the legendary "Ghan" to see how it compares to the Orient Express.

Day Twenty-five

We enjoyed the unexpected extra day that we had in Sydney by wasting a large percentage of it getting up later than we intended. We strolled to the nearest Starbucks for breakfast; I am never disappointed with a Starbucks cappuccino with extra chocolate. Now whilst I think about it, I really wish I had shares in said coffee shop, as I had a sneaking suspicion that by the end of our journey we would have visited an awful lot of Starbucks around the world. She (that is to say me) who was often prone to a little bit of exaggeration on this occasion was not; David could confirm that my increasing waistline was testimony to that fact. Just to finish on that topic, I came to the conclusion very early on the best ones were in the United Kingdom, the food is better, offering greater selection, and if you drink in you get a china mug and not a flimsy paper cup.

After breakfast, we made our way to Hyde Park Barracks Museum. The museum was a beautiful piece of architecture and has played many roles since being built from 1817–19. From 1819 to 1848 it was a barracks designed to provide secure night lodging for government assigned male convicts. From 1848 to 1886 it became the immigration depot for single females. The central dormitory building was altered, and iron beds replaced hammocks. From 1862 to 1886 a new government asylum for aged, infirm, and destitute women was established on one of the levels. From 1887 to 1979, a

My Travels with Wheely

major programme of works was undertaken to create courts and government offices. From 1979 to the present day, it has been a museum.

Unfortunately, I was unable to get the real feel of what this building was like as there was no wheelchair access for getting upstairs. Instead, they very kindly showed me a model of the museum that came apart and showed me the building in detail. They also had some artefacts, which included some of the clothes actually worn by the prisoners. We wore special gloves and were able to touch them, which I found incredible as it was something to be preserved. It was all so well presented it gave you a real insight as to what it was like when it was a prison. They also allowed me to experience something other people did not, and I was grateful.

Once again, we found ourselves walking through the botanical gardens on what was yet another glorious day, not a cloud in the sky. The plants were enormous and I took a picture of David amongst the plants, making it look as though he was in the jungle. The thing it lacked to make it really convincing was a machete.

Like magnets, we found ourselves being drawn toward the opera house for one final glimpse. This time we walked around the harbour to somewhere called The Rocks for different views and yet more photographs. This also enabled David to take more photographs of what had become his beloved Harbour Bridge; we watched with envy people walking over the bridge and wished we could do the same.

Nicky Dalladay

Having returned to the hotel it was time to repack our belongings in readiness for our departure in the morning. My heart broke yet again seeing David doing everything. I hated to think how much he would be doing this in the near future, so I didn't think about it, and my thoughts turned to my stomach and wondered where we should go for dinner tonight. Who knows, perhaps I shall be referring to myself in the very near future as Mrs. Golightly.

Darling Harbour beckoned once more and with the same indecision as previously encountered we once again spent some time seeking out the restaurant where we would like to dine. We settled for the Meat and Wine Company and ate lots of lovely steak. Jolly delicious it was too.

My goodness, I saw a very rare sight: a bloke multitasking, which is definitely worth a mention because I personally have never seen this phenomenon before. He was talking on his mobile, eating, and smoking. How clever was he?

E-mails Received

Dear DallAwayDays, (like it) Sounds as though you are getting many different experiences, to say the least, which I know you will relish. Anyway, you sound cheerful enough, despite the lack of alcohol! S&AM

We love getting your updates. Perth sounds ghastly and we won't be going there! Saw a programme about grotesquely fat people last night; we're now on a starvation diet. You're missing some stunning grey days here; sun is most definitely

My Travels with Wheely

staying with you in Australia. NB

Astonishingly enough we have *not* yet set off the alarm who would have thought that! Your experiences sound so exiting; I enjoy reading the e-mails and am so happy you are having a wonderful time. The two of you deserve this. MK

Darling DallAwayDays, it's not the greatest of impressions of Oz from your first few days. However in your other e-mail you did say that the Vietnamese made you feel big so after Perth and Scarborough Beach, you must be thinking of yourself as nice and slim. Sydney sounds more like it though, and I do hope that you both got enough alcohol, what's life without booze! Keep your e-mails coming; it all sounds very exciting, if exhausting. M &JG

Great to hear you're having a good time. Love to be sharing your trip in person but your reports are the next best thing. Poor old David it's hard to believe that there's no beer in Perth. I thought that Oz was the home of macho, beer-swilling Bruces but they're clearly just a bunch of wimps. RA

It is so refreshing to hear your experiences, especially as I look out of the window at a typical grey and dim February day in England. So glad you're having a great time. Look forward to hearing about your adventures; that is the only way we get to travel these days. KD

It all sounds amazing so far, as good as you thought it might be, I guess. I hope you don't mind, but I have been forwarded your news. I can tell you both that as far as weather is concerned you are not missing a thing. I look

Nicky Dalladay

forward to hearing more; I especially love the humour, Nicky! TH

Really enjoying your e-mails and I'm so pleased that, apart from Perth, all seems to be going well. You missed some very cold weather here last week it was -two. DM was in the office last week and gave me an update of your activities as he'd seen you in Bangkok. DJ

I hope that you don't mind my interrupting your adventures but it has taken some time to get around to e-mailing and had to ask DJ for your e-mail address. I hope that is okay. Tell me to buzz off if not. Have seen In Transit Singapore message and followed your trips into Vietnam and Bangkok using Google image to look at where you are. It looks absolutely fantastic. I expect you are now fully into Australia as that was a week ago. Really glad you are enjoying it, although a little concerned regarding the bathing arrangements in Vietnam and it being so hot. Hope you managed a good scrub down at some stage! Much the same here though, Cold, cold, and more cold and looking forward to the spring as I have a few challenges to complete this year, including an Olympic distance triathlon in June, yep still doing mad things. Shouldn't let old blokes like me out in lycra but hey, what the hell, I had a couple of girls hoot at me, think I was probably in the way but in any case it gives my ego a boost! SS

Just reading about your escapades makes me tired. It's good to hear you sounding in such good form. It's strange really when I recall you talking about the Far East and your concerns about it and yet Perth sounds more

My Travels with Wheely

backward and uncivilized than those places! GH

Darlings, there is nothing wrong with petrol stations wherever they are situated in the world. Personally, I find them rather attractive! Yet another fantastic update. Thanks for including me and keep them coming. AA

Dear Dull Ladies, Glad you're having a good time. Five hundred pictures … mm. Hope you remembered to turn the camera the other way up while in Oz. P&CF

Thanks for your updates and especially for warning us about Perth. I'll never darken its abstemious door. As I'm sure others have told you, the weather here has been bad. So think of that and enjoy. J&JW

Dear Dallydaze, Sheila, you're in Australia now so don't go bleating on about feelings, if you don't like it you can bugger off back home, you Limey! By the way have you mentioned that we won the Ashes? You have! You are so harsh. It's so lovely to hear from you again. EA

How lovely to have so many e-mail messages from home. However, I am somewhat concerned that we seem to have a lot of alcoholic friends. Then there are those who have missed their vocation in life on the meteorological front.

Day Twenty-six
Flight Eight, Sydney to Ayers Rock

Left the lovely Sydney behind, which we were quite sad about, to make our way to the airport, a mere twenty-minute taxi ride away; our next destination was Ayers Rock. It was about a three-hour flight.

Near to the end of our flight I decided to use the toilet and on the way back the "trolley dolley" invited us to sit in business class. She proceeded to tell us to sit on the left and to be ready for the beautiful view, the Rock of course. We were not disappointed. Wow, it was truly awesome, and we once again pinched ourselves. Were we really seeing this? Yes of course we were, but it looked very small from up here.

A catastrophe happened, which, according to the pessimist David, he supposed was inevitable at some point. My poor trusted Wheely arrived in the arrival hall looking like a somewhat mangled heap and a shadow of his former self. I was furious; it just showed how insensitive and uncaring people could be about personal possessions. As I stated previously, one is not much use without the other, and never more so than right now. The thing that angered me most was the lack of respect the handling staff had for my property and didn't consider just how important and necessary some belongings are. Obviously, the handling staff didn't need to avail themselves of a wheelchair, lucky them, and therefore as far as I was concerned they didn't

My Travels with Wheely

give a monkey's.

A report was completed and we were informed they could do nothing; after all, this was the middle of nowhere. Boy how right they were. They thought that perhaps they could send it off to Adelaide to be repaired and meet me us in Darwin, but the chances of that working smoothly were very slim, according to the resident pessimist — sorry, I meant realist — David. So it was decided that the best option would be to take Wheely to the hotel and let them see if they could do anything, and deal with a claim back in London.

So the airport provided us with one of their wheelchairs to get me to the hotel. Well, if I'd weighed in at twenty stone — thankfully I didn't, not yet anyway — it would have fitted me perfectly, with plenty of room to spare. A rather interesting feature of this very large wheelchair was the pneumatic tyres. What do pneumatic tyres need? They need to have air in them. It seemed that the essential ingredient, air, was missing. Did they have a pump anywhere? Did they hell.

By now, largely due to the inordinate amount of time this has taken, we had missed two transfer coaches to the hotel, so we sat outside and contemplated until the arrival of the next one; we hadn't really noticed the flies much.

Finally we arrived at the hotel, and poor Wheely disappeared to the sick bay/maintenance department. I swear I could see a tear a roll down his arm. Forgive me for being pessimistic — this is normally reserved for David — but I thought that there was a strong possibility he would

Nicky Dalladay

probably come back to me in the same condition he left me. He did … god how I hated to be right. This incident temporarily satisfied David and supported his view that a pessimist could never be disappointed, and that I, as an optimist, could only ever set myself up to be disappointed. Whilst deliberating the differences of our natures, I hated having to remind him that Wheely was still on death's door.

David went to visit the sick bay/maintenance department to see just what tools they had. Armed with a crowbar he gently levered the seat bar as much as he dared in order to get the seat into its almost proper position. We were now able to use Wheely again although rather carefully and with a lot more respect.

This whole event upset me somewhat particularly, watching David and the amount of work he had to do. It just highlighted to me just how useless I had become. Back in the days when I used to reside in the able-bodied world, I never had feelings like this. How I hated having them now; part of me had gotten lost somewhere. This episode pointed out again the enormity of just what he had to do, and I really don't think I took any of this on board when we embarked on this journey. Oddly, David didn't worry about it and said, "It's just one of those things." Hang on a second. This was not a pessimist speaking. Had he transferred from the dark side?

On a serious note, I took my hat off to him; after all these years I could honestly say that I hadn't appreciated just how much emotional strength he had. Hopefully the day would get better.

My Travels with Wheely

We eventually got to our room in this supposedly five-star hotel. I'd seriously like to know how this establishment was rated; since there was no way it was good enough for five stars. It was more like two and a bit. Anyway, we went and sat on the patio. Well, when I said patio I actually didn't quite mean that … the area we were in resembled a crossroads because there was a constant flurry of activity. So we sat there with a drink and acknowledged all the passersby, I imagined that this was pretty much like a holiday camp and it was only now that we really noticed the flies.

Just sitting there reminded me of the television programme *The Prisoner*. It wasn't only the buildings and the layout but the little buggies that the staff drove around in, and I was half expecting Patrick McGoohan to appear being chased by a ball.

I had never experienced the amount of flies present there, and I hope I never will again. It was just disgusting, and no amount of waving your arms around would keep them away, they just stuck to your face. It reminded me very much of watching footage from Africa where there were flies absolutely everywhere.

We made a speedy getaway from the flies and went into the hotel to find out what our package included. We were informed it was a Sounds of Silence Dinner — oh how intriguing — couldn't wait to find out what that was all about. Whilst on our journey we had decided to embrace as many new experiences as possible. If we didn't do it now, when would we? With that in mind, we then went to book a helicopter flight. Well why on Earth not? This was a once-in-a-lifetime opportunity.

Nicky Dalladay

Tonight, was the Sounds of Silence Dinner, and we were picked up from our hotel and taken to a location a few miles from the Rock, which now looked enormous. It just shows you how being on a plane can distort the size.

We found ourselves in the romance of the desert viewing the setting of the sun behind the domes of Kata Tjuta, and it was perfect. There was a beautiful reception where champagne and canapés were served, and we tasted our first kangaroo, emu, and crocodile, which were delectable. The gentle or should I say haunting tones of the didgeridoo were being played in the background whether we liked it or not, and it was part of the evening and very fitting. We were shown to the exquisite dining area and shared a table with Jo and Hal, who were from Chattanooga, and Martha and Larry who were from Ontario. The company was delightful.

The evening warmth and stillness was blissful and the view of the Rock was just amazing. Perhaps I should have the decency to refer to it by its proper name: Uluru, on one side, and Kata Tjuta on the other. We'd never heard of Kata Tjuta before, and it equalled the size of Uluru. But it was not complete (I guess that's why it doesn't receive the same billing); nonetheless, it was indeed beautiful. The only real shame was it was cloudy; a clear night would have been breathtaking, but you can't have everything.

After we ate I asked the table if they minded if I had a cigarette, which they all said was fine, so I lit up. Before I knew it a waiter pounced on me and said that this was a no-smoking area. Somewhat flabbergasted, I said, "But we are outside." He proceeded to reel off Australian legislation

My Travels with Wheely

and rules and informed me that it was in fact illegal to smoke at the table and that should I wish to smoke I would have to go to the designated smoking area twenty feet away, by which time I had finished my cigarette and that was that.

All in all, it was a fabulous evening. We tasted the delights of many dishes we had never had the chance to try before, and the setting was stunning. Amazingly enough, at sunset the flies disappeared to go and annoy someone or something else. Great, at last there was some respite.

Before we left, Martha gave me her and Larry's e-mail addresses. They were such a wonderful couple I hoped our paths would cross again in the future. We arrived back at the hotel slightly worse for drink, but hey, we had just had an amazing experience.

Nicky Dalladay

Sounds of Silence Dinner

Day Twenty-seven
First Helicopter Flight

We woke bleary eyed, and dare I say a little hung over. Today we were going to be picked up and taken to the heliport for our flight, which should last for about thirty-six minutes. It's not me, it was advertised as the length of time it would last for. We had booked the extended Uluru and Kata Tjuta flight to allow us plenty of time to take lots of photographs.

At the heliport, the three of us decided upon the best strategy for getting me into the helicopter. It was not easy, but after a bit of pushing and shoving, I was finally in. We waved goodbye to Wheely, who had to sit on the tarmac and wait dutifully for our return. The excitement was twofold; first, we were in a helicopter, and second, we were about to fly over one of the natural wonders of the world.

Up, up, and away, we flew over the desert, where you were afforded the merest glimpse of this vast expanse of wilderness; this really is a very big country. We saw camels, which took me completely by surprise, not really sure why as it was the desert. The land looked very barren and desolate, but David and I were staggered by the richness of the dark red colour. The day was just glorious, and we were flown over Ayers Rock and Kata Tjuta. It was usual to see this sort of magnificence on television, but we were actually there, up in the air, and living our dream. Did we appreciate just how privileged we were? Yes, we certainly did; one can never take anything for granted in this life. I do regret very much that I just don't have the words to describe this experience. It was just so miraculous, you really had to see it to believe it, and we pinched ourselves once more.

We got back to the hotel and were just roasting. I'd never been so hot. We wandered aimlessly, not quite sure what to do with ourselves; we were melting and the flies were back.

I am very conscious that I have made quite a lot of reference to the heat and feel that a little explanation is required. I used to adore the sun and the hot weather, but now I find that my body just won't tolerate it. The heat has become a great inconvenience to me by debilitating my body and depriving me of the little strength that I have. My legs and feet swell to such proportions you could be forgiven for likening me to a rhino, without the horn of course. I'm sure you get the picture. Attractive, eh? I am certainly not complaining but just really stating a fact about one of the changes I have had to get used to.

Enough of that; where were we? We retreated to the room; I really can't tell you just how horrible the flies were. I went to the bathroom but for some reason the legs and feet weren't on Wheely, and David pulled me out of the bathroom by my feet. Before we knew it, bang! I've landed on my head. Ouch, it really hurt and David felt extremely bad about it. Secretly I think the Wheely episode had really got to him, and he was trying to kill me.

Day Twenty-eight
Flight Nine

We took an early morning flight to Alice Springs, which proved to be just as hot as Ayers Rock, but at least there weren't as many flies. We sat by the pool for a while to catch our breath before walking into town. On the way, we crossed a river. We only knew it was a river because there was a sign on it that served as a very good clue: the River Adelaide. But there was no water in it; in fact, it was bone dry. Whilst it amused us, the lack of rainfall in the core of the country was a very serious problem. We were subsequently informed that it did fill up three times a year, which must be a cause for much celebration and jubilation. I tried to imagine it as a river and came to the conclusion that it would look just fantastic, but we were in the dry season and there was certainly no rain forecast. The river demonstrated how dry and arid the heart of Australia is. It was here that you realised how lush and green home really is.

The hotel was very kind and furnished us with an Alice Springs town map so we could at least try and find our way around and look for a suitable restaurant. Goodness me, what choices! There was McDonalds, KFC, or the Red Rooster. Being the international travellers we now were, we decided the aforementioned "restaurants" were not for us. We remembered that on our way into town we had passed a very interesting looking restaurant, so

Nicky Dalladay

without delay or more dithering we headed to the only real contender, the Blue Grass Restaurant. It was on the roadside, and that was possibly why we had dismissed it in the first place. The fact that it lay beside the road is hardly worth mentioning really, as only one car passed us all evening. David dined on a kangaroo steak, and I had a fillet steak, and he was so happy that he bounced all the way back to the hotel.

E-mails Received

I have given up attempting to place where you are exactly at a given time. As I am away tomorrow night I do not have any alternative but to send you birthday greetings now, Nicky, in the hope that they will reach you as close to your special day as possible. How was the train journey? Is it really a special one? Does it have the same aura of appeal as the Orient Express? Is that asking too much of Oz? How are you bearing up with all the hardship of … travel, food and wine, sunny weather, different cultures, meeting new people? Envy oozes out from every pore! R&GD

VM kindly sent on missive number three once she worked out that we weren't on the mailing list and was fed up of us asking how you were both getting on. 7 February was J's birthday: he declined my offer of a meal out in favour of the bridge club. However the cards weren't at all nice, so J was not a happy birthday bunny. Today it's raining. What's new you might say, but in fact we haven't had any rain for six weeks apparently, so we're all giving thanks to the rain god. Bet you're enjoying some lovely weather. Thinking of you both, have a brilliant time. We're already

My Travels with Wheely

looking forward to the photos (sad gits that we are). JB

I would like it if you put me on your regular updates, sounds like you are getting around and seeing lots. Everything fine here but I don't think it has rained since you left until today that is and there are dark rumours of water shortages in the summer if we don't get a shed load of rain over the next couple of months, we will have to wait and see. Enjoy the sunshine down under. JRB

More messages from home. Oh, I had nearly forgotten it would be my birthday soon, and of course we received the weather update; how very useful that was?

Day Twenty-nine

Due to leave the hotel today but we managed to wangle an extension on our departure. It's good that we got this as David has had to repack and work a few miracles on the baggage front. We were due to board the Ghan train and are restricted to one small bag. Finally, we were ready to set off for the station. Naturally we were in good time, but you'd expect nothing less with David as he still insisted on getting everywhere excessively early. It has been duly noted, however, that this doesn't extend to getting out of bed earlier.

Departed Alice Springs and I couldn't say I was particularly sorry; it wasn't the prettiest of places. Alice seemed to house half the aborigine population, who appeared to be quite content doing nothing and sitting on their derrières drinking. They seemed oblivious to the fact that they lived in a community, and they seemingly did nothing toward making a contribution to society whatsoever. Add to this they were a miserable bunch of people. Finally, we were rid of those pesky flies.

We arrived at the station to board the Ghan. No, sorry … I should have said the Legendary Ghan Train. Incidentally the taxi driver who dropped us off said he couldn't see why anyone would want to do this boring twenty-four-hour journey through the outback. Nice to hear those words of encouragement when you are about to embark on a long journey.

My Travels with Wheely

We proceeded with going through the ticketing business, with them relieving us of most of our donkey train, and we were just left with one small bag. We walked along the entire platform to have a look at the train that housed many carriages. I had no idea how many there were but suffice it to say, there were an awful lot. All the carriages, with the exception of one, were silver whilst the main carriage at the front was bright red. It all looked very impressive, and we couldn't wait to get on and start our journey.

So bearing that in mind, all that was left for us to do was now board the train which proved easier said than done. We looked at the width of the carriage doorway and at the width of Wheely and thought, *Hang on a second* … it looked very much as though we wouldn't fit. Whilst scratching our chins and wondering how I was going to get on the train, the answer came trundling around the corner. By the look of it, this was about to turn out to be one of the most novel and some might say interesting experiences of getting on a train. The thing that was trundling around the corner was a fork lift truck.

We are all too well aware of the fact that we now live in a society governed by political correctness; the world has gone quite mad. Not here it hadn't. A very kind gentleman proceeded to load me as if I were a box of precious China and deposited me on the train.

After being boarded they had to help me transfer to an aisle chair, and as it transpired, the width of the corridors on the train would be too narrow for Wheely. So not for the first time, we said goodbye to Wheely and hoped we

Nicky Dalladay

would be reunited in due course.

Hardly glamorous, but they at least got me on the train in one piece. Still, it's yet another mode of transport I could add to my ever increasing list. With all passengers safely on board, the train departed at precisely 16.00.

We were shown to our compartment, and we were lucky because being disabled the accommodation was larger than the non disabled compartments. Blimey, you could barely swing a cat in ours — I would love to see what theirs was like. Luckily for us, we had the foresight to upgrade ourselves to the Gold Kangaroo service.

Having been privileged to have travelled on the Orient Express, I rather expected the Legendary Ghan to be very similar, but it wasn't; it merely demonstrated once more how the Australians seem to have no class.

It was interesting, however, to learn about some of the Ghan's history. Originally the Afghan Express, the name Ghan was inspired by the pioneering Afghan cameleers who blazed a permanent trail into the Red Centre of Australia more than one hundred fifty years ago. The Ghan's emblem is an Afghan on a camel in recognition of their efforts in opening up the inhospitable interior to the rest of Australia.

Well we had such fun in the twenty-four hours and met some smashing people, so the journey was not boring in the slightest. We felt humble to be able to take this ultimate journey through the very heart of the Australian continent.

My Travels with Wheely

It is a well known fact that amongst the remaining smokers in this world you can get to meet some of the most interesting people ever. These days smoking areas tend to be small and naturally full of fog and like-minded people who enjoy having a cigarette, and this was no exception. We had a beautiful dinner on board; after which we adjourned to the bar for a swift beer. At 22.30 we were literally sent to bed as we'd be woken up at 06.30.

Boarding The Legendary Ghan

Day Thirty
Second Helicopter Flight

Today it was St. Valentine's Day and my birthday, and as promised we were woken at 06.30 with the dulcet tones of good morning, coffee, etc. The train was due to stop for a couple of hours and there were numerous trips to go on, but most of them required mobility skills, so they were out of the question. There was only one thing we could do, and that was a helicopter flight, what a shame. So we took to the skies once more for our second helicopter flight of the trip. We had decided to take the scenic flight over all thirteen Katherine Gorges and Nitmiluk National Park, which promised frequent sightings of local wildlife. We think they must all have been asleep as we didn't see any. The Katherine Gorge with its beautiful scenery was a very good start to my birthday on what was yet another sweltering day.

We were escorted back to the train in time for lunch, and I was presented a bottle of Champagne — or rather, sparkling wine — and the carriage sang happy birthday to me. It was all rather sweet and much unexpected; I was immensely touched and taken aback. I collected a few names and addresses and would like to think I would keep in touch, but who knows.

We disembarked the train at just after 16.30 and were taken to our hotel in Darwin. We were shown to a

Nicky Dalladay

junior suite, which was large enough for us to rethink the packing, sort out the laundry, and collect our thoughts. Tears filled my eyes. There was the most beautiful bouquet of flowers from our closest friends, together with a token for a beauty treatment. How clever of them and oh so kind. Other people had also sent birthday cards and I had a few given to me before we left and set about opening all of those. It reminded me just how lucky we were and it was heart warming to know that although we were out of sight we were definitely not out of mind. Shortly afterward, we ventured out to look for a restaurant. This was the best birthday ever!

E-mails Received

This is just a quickie to wish you many happy returns for your birthday tomorrow, although it's probably today already wherever you are. I've just come back to work after a week off and full of the joys of spring, not! I hope that you are still enjoying the holiday and are not drinking too much. Enjoy the heat, it's been freezing here for the last couple of weeks, a bit milder today but alas, raining. CB

Imagine heavenly voices (well, me and S actually), clearing throats, coughing, you get the picture. Now slowing building Happy birthday to you, happy birthday to you, happy birthday dear Nicky, happy birthday toooooooooo (big finish) YOU. Are you fed up with it all yet? The sun, sea, etc. No, we didn't think so. Hope you're both well and everything is going to plan. We are missing you both loads. S&GM

My Travels with Wheely

What an adventure! I can't wait to hear more details. When do you arrive in Hawaii? It sounds like you are doing really well. Can't believe the wedding is almost here. Really looking forward to seeing you and meeting your husband! Have a safe journey. CJ

Dear Nick, Happy Birthday 2 U. Hope that our cards arrived in time. AC

Hope you're having a fantastic birthday and hope you aren't somewhere where it was yesterday and so this is late. I am so sorry if this is the case. C&NB

Wherever you are and whatever you are doing, today is the 14 February, and so … happy birthday, dear Nicky, happy birthday to you. AA

Just to wish you a very happy birthday, Nicky. I am sure the scenery where you are is better than the view I've got, i.e. Romford. Look forward to your next instalment. R&LA

Many thanks for your update No three. You will obviously have moved on by now: to where? Are you still in Australia? Oh goody, loads more photos to see.… Hope you are having a great time … think of us in the cold and rain. VM

Happy Birthday. Hope you are both having the time of your lives. We are green with envy. Keep the progress reports coming, we are all eyes. PL

I hope you are having a great birthday wherever you may be. Also hoping you are enjoying it a little more

Nicky Dalladay

than Perth, it didn't sound like you thought that much of it! Everything is pretty much as normal here, weather miserable. Looking forward to reading your next instalment. JS

Just to reiterate the point: yes, my birthday is on Valentine's Day. I wish I had a romantic name to go with it. A name change is rather appealing, perhaps something like "Valentina." Mm, Valentina Dalladay well, why not? You could have numerous made-up names these days. I would have to give it some thought.

Day Thirty-one

With my birthday celebrations firmly behind us I had now notched up another year. Not that that makes any difference — you are as old as you feel — and what's in a number?

We consulted the map to establish our bearings and decided we would walk to Cullen Bay. We were not disappointed with our randomly chosen destination; it was, in fact, a most delightful place, but rather sadly most of it seemed to be closed. Of course we had been informed at this time of year the Northern territories were now well and truly in the wet season, and with the wet season, apparently virtually everything closes. When making our plans we were aware that we would be going through many climactic regions, in some places we would encounter wonderful weather and in some we wouldn't. However, not to be deterred by inclement weather like a little drop of rain, we soldiered on and were rewarded for our tenacity. We found just one restaurant open, which fortunately for us was very nice, and stopped for a quick bite to eat and a swift beer. A taxi ride back was necessary, because as we so often do we walked further than originally intended and it was just too far to walk — or, more accurately, for David to push.

Now back where we started, we headed off in the other direction to Stokes Hill Wharf, which quite frankly was rather dull. It was a very grey-looking place, and we found ourselves walking through some sort of construction site,

Nicky Dalladay

although we eventually made our way to the pier. There wasn't a lot open, and we just assumed that was because it was the wet season. As if to punctuate it was the wet season, the heavens proceeded to open and heave it down. It reminded us of when were in Stanley, Hong Kong, because it was just as torrential as it was then. We were soaked through but were laughing. Fortunately, neither of us are fair-weather people, which was just as well under the circumstances. We sought refuge under the only covered area there was, which just so happened to be a shop. It was, in fact, a pearl and shell shop. Rather ironically, I bought a paua shell heart pendant that comes from New Zealand. I could have actually waited until we got there to make a purchase, but no, my motto is to buy when you see something you like.

E-mail Received

I meant to send a message yesterday to wish you a very happy birthday. (I won't even begin to explain why I didn't manage to, other than to say the usual cr@p here that takes over my life!) Are you sending out tickets to those who want to book in for the photo viewings? Keep keeping in touch; it really is great to hear about your trip. WR

This was some evidence of work seriously getting in the way of life; luckily, this was one thing we were no longer concerned with.

Day Thirty-two

Darwin was a fabulous place to be in for a few days. There was a wealth of activity available. A bit more excitement for the day: we joined the jumping crocodile tour. Well, why not? We had nothing better to do. We had already eaten them, so we might just as well see them for real. The day consisted of a boat trip (obviously, since we were looking for crocodiles); we journeyed up the river in search of them. We were on the famous Adelaide River Jumping Crocodile Cruise; how cool was this? We remained confused as to how this could possibly be the Adelaide River as we were nowhere near Adelaide but decided not to dwell on this too much.

Using pork tied to string, our guide enticed the crocodiles to leap out of the water, which enabled us to see these prehistoric creatures at close range. Then we came across the mother of all crocodiles, as the saying goes, and his name apparently was Agro. He was six and a half metres in length with a girth of two metres. We watched him being fed, and my goodness, what a big mouth he had! The size of each tooth was just huge; it was just incredible that you could get so close to something like this. We also saw Seahawks being fed as well, and Magpie Geese, who rather strangely looked like Magpies in a gooselike way.

The tour was an exceptional one and certainly not one to be missed; it had a real novelty value. The woman

Nicky Dalladay

giving the tour had the most peculiar accent I'd ever heard, and because she referred to the township in the Northern Territory, and given the way she spoke, I assumed she was South African. Silly me, she was, in fact, French, and I'd never have guessed that in a million years. Her parents were French and she had been brought up in Paris, so I deduced she must have learned her English from a South African.

They were very politically correct here, which really got my goat. They actually changed the name of the White-breasted bird to the White-chested bird. I ask you, was that not truly ridiculous? The woman who was telling us this thought it was madness, and it had been suggested that they were planning on rethinking the name of the Cockatoo.

Day Thirty-three

I rose fairly late this morning after an abysmal night's sleep. The alien had reappeared. How dare it come back uninvited into my life? We eventually got out of the hotel and headed for a late breakfast. Today I was going to have my beauty treatment; I didn't suppose they would have sufficient time to give me a completely new face, so I would have to settle for what they could do. David took me to the beauty salon where I selected from the service menu, as they called it, a detoxifying facial, a refreshing foot soak and massage (yes, my feet and ankles were still very swollen and hideous), and finally an eyebrow shape. Whilst I was undergoing major reconstruction, or being pampered, as it is more commonly referred to, courtesy of my lovely friends, David felt it was time to get to grips with the laundry again, and went in search of the guest laundry room. Now beautified, I emerged a new woman and we went out for a swift beer and a light supper.

We got a chance to see if we had any e-mails, and there was a very strange one saying it hoped we enjoyed the surprise. What surprise? we wondered. The only surprise there was that there wasn't one. Anyway, we eventually got to the bottom of it, and it transpired that contact had been made directly with the hotel. This was now where it all fell apart; it had been incorrectly assumed that we would dine in the hotel on 14 February at their special Valentine's dinner.

Nicky Dalladay

For us, life has had to change beyond all recognition. We no longer enjoyed cosy meals for two. It's an extremely romantic day to have a birthday, but we didn't feel the need to share the evening with lots of strangers to demonstrate our love for each other; we had that in abundance, and an overpriced meal would certainly not change the way we felt about each other. In the old capable days I felt differently, and of course being able to use cutlery was a distinct advantage. Don't get me wrong; I'm romantic at heart, and I suppose what I'm alluding to is that now I'd prefer to have a birthday sharing it with our friends who are used to my eating habits and me wearing most of my food. No pleasing some people, is there? Although the surprise didn't come off it was such a lovely gesture and very thoughtful.

Day Thirty-four

Today we purchased a tube of toothpaste, which demonstrated to us just how long we had been away. This gave me quite an odd feeling as it was the first time we had ever experienced being away from home for more than a couple of weeks. So, we had now been away for just over a month and had to buy a tube of toothpaste, but in a flash, "professor" David quite rightly pointed out that this was a much bigger tube and should last longer. However, the jury was still out on that one; see what I have to put up with?

This was, in fact, our last day in Darwin, and as a little treat for David, I suggested we go to the Aviation Heritage Centre. We decided to get a bus there just for the experience and made our way to the bus stop; obviously we got our kicks in strange ways. Rather bizarrely there was a no-smoking sign at the bus stop. We were in a road open to the elements and clearly you could smoke all the way around it but not at it. I always thought the Australians were a little crazy; in one fell swoop they had confirmed my suspicions.

Anyway, back to the real issue, we arrived at the Aviation Centre, where David suddenly transformed into a school boy and became wildly excited, as he was in his element. Did I know he was touching the massive Boeing B-52 bomber, which was one of only two on display in the world outside the USA? Yes I did, because he had told

Nicky Dalladay

me several times. I didn't quite share his enthusiasm, but this moment was not about me, it was about him actually seeing something of interest to him. I then proceeded to take several pictures of him by, under, wherever he wished with the B-52, and he was now very content.

I left him to look around the rest of the centre and went outside for a cigarette. Whilst I was out there I was chatting with somebody who worked there, and he told me the other B-52 was in a little place called Duxford, United Kingdom, and had I heard of it? I just laughed and said yes I had.

The remainder of the day was spent wandering around Darwin and us purchasing our second bottle of mouthwash. It was the same size as before, and David made no comment as to how long it should last, thank god for that.

We went out for supper and found a lovely place to eat. It had an Irish theme and the table mats kept us quite amused for some time. They were just pieces of paper with anecdotes on them. One of them was about Murphy's Law: "Anything that can go wrong, will go wrong," and funnily enough David had that one.

Mine was about the phenomenal power of the human mind which read as follows:

Aoccdrnig to a rseecharer at Cmabrigde Uinervtisy, it deosn't mttaer in waht order the ltteers in a wrod are the olny iprmoatnt tihng is taht the frist and lsat ltteer be in the rghit pclae. The rset can be a taotl mses and you can sitll raed it wouthit porblem. Tiihs is bcuseae the huamn

My Travels with Wheely

mind deos not raed ervey lteter by istlef, but the wrod as a wlohe.

That has to be one of the most difficult paragraphs I have ever had to type. We had a lovely evening but were mindful of the fact that we needed to have an early night in readiness for our very early morning wake-up call.

Fourth E-mail

Once upon a time there were two pom travellers… ah, yes, now I remember where I was. We were just embarking for the Blue Mountains. We were outside the hotel, ready and waiting to be picked up, when Max our tour guide bounds up to us and says, are you Mr. & Mrs. Dalladay? Why yes, we reply, and Max then says, blimey nobody told me you were in a wheelchair, can you walk? If I could f****** walk I wouldn't be in this contraption! Max then informs us that he is a paramedic. Not quite sure what to make of that but have no doubt it will prove useful at some point.

Anyway, we are now making our way toward the mountains. It's overcast, hot, and steamy but beautiful, and we see kangaroos and kookaburras, etc. The scenery was spectacular and quite breathtaking. There was one area that was very tricky to get to and Max said he and David could chair lift me down. Now in theory that sounds like a good idea, but he was six feet, four inches, and as you know David is not quite that tall (five feet eight and a bit); anyway, they did it, and boy the view was indeed awesome.

We stayed at a beautiful hotel in the mountains for the

Nicky Dalladay

night and consumed a low-fat high tea followed by an equally low-fat cheese for supper with wine and port. Jolly yummy it was too.

Back to Sydney for another couple of days, with some time spent in the botanical gardens and a few beers without food for David in the middle of the afternoon; what a happy bunny he was.

Out to Darling Harbour for dinner and a huge choice of restaurants, I think I forgot to mention I was on the verge of becoming a vegetarian especially after Vietnam, but then we hit upon the Meat & Wine Restaurant and of my thoughts went with the big fat juicy steak. My sincere apologies to all of you veggies.

From Sydney we flew to Ayers Rock, as we were reliably informed there was this little rock in the middle of nowhere to see. On arrival at AR we had some catastrophic news: Wheely suffered at the hands of Quantas and came limping out the door somewhat bent…poor Wheely. It was a sad moment indeed. We were given an inferior wheelchair, not even worthy of a name, to use. Poor Wheely accompanied us to the hotel to be attended to at the Wheely hospital. Where's Max when you need him? Ah, the trusty David has his spanners and goes to seek assistance to try and un-mangle the seat. Wheely is now covered with various brightly coloured plasters (duct tape) but reasonably straightened out.

We can confirm that yes, it is in the middle of absolutely nowhere, and oh yes, it is big! You'll no doubt be pleased to learn that we do in fact have several pictures

My Travels with Wheely

around and above the Rock from a helicopter. The most memorable wildlife of the area was the flies, which were persistently annoying, and we can see why the corks on the end of the hat are not just to make you look stupid but are also quite essential. The only good thing about it was that there were no dogs around — therefore, no dog s***! We cannot tell you how horrid it was. This was a truly amazing experience and one that we had only seen in books or on TV. Boy how lucky are we?

We were at the rock for two days and on our first night went to a Sounds of Silence Dinner, location in view of the Rock, of course. It was the most beautiful evening, done in such style with a reception area out in the open for a drop or two of champagne, and a sumptuous dinner consisting of crocodile and kangaroo.

We left Ayers Rock to fly to Alice Springs, where we saw the whole population of aborigines, or so it seemed. They do absolutely nothing apart from sit and drink and get paid by the government for doing very little; apparently, they are a protected race. They can be described as having rather unique and some might even say distinctive features. Not a lot goes on in Alice. There are a lot of rivers but all without water, so it seems a little strange to call them rivers, although we were reliably informed it does rain at least three times a year.

Haven't really made reference to the weather yet but believe me it has been seriously hot, upper thirties the whole time, and such a beautiful blue sky like we've never seen, largely because there are no clouds.

Nicky Dalladay

The reason that we went to AS was so that we could board the train referred to as "The Legendary Ghan." We're not entirely sure why it is legendary because they only completed the track from AS to Darwin in 2004, and "class and no" spring to mind. Having been fortunate enough to have stayed overnight on the even-more-legendary Orient Express, we rather assumed it would be similar. Shows how wrong you can be.

The journey gave us a real insight into just how big this country is. It's quite unbelievable that you can travel for so long and not see a thing, just a mass of green and brown land. It was a good opportunity to talk to fellow travellers and meet some wonderful people.

We made a stop just short of Darwin at a place called Katherine. The only trip on offer we could make was a helicopter flight over the gorges, which was beautiful and so green. When we re-boarded the train for lunch we had a lovely surprise: "Happy Birthday" sung by the carriage and a bottle of something fizzy. What a lovely way to start my birthday.

It's 14 February, I'm another year older, and we arrive in Darwin. Thank you so much for the lovely text messages, e-mails, cards, and presents. You're all lovely people, and I had the most memorable birthday ever.

By the way, Darwin seems to be home to the rest of the aborigines. Darwin is beautiful but very quiet. We have arrived in the wet season. *Wet season*, we say to ourselves. It's so hot and blue and — oops, it's just started to heave it down, but it soon clears. On our first day we went to

My Travels with Wheely

Cullen Bay because there were some beautiful restaurants there, but as it was the wet season there was only one open.

We have just "chilled" for a couple of days, which has been lovely; we have been on a short trip to the Adelaide River, which is nowhere near Adelaide, for a jumping crocodile cruise. It was yet another memorable experience.

We leave Darwin tonight to go to Port Douglas, and we will try and do another short e-mail next week before leaving for NZ.

Love to everyone
The DallAwayDays
xxxx

Day Thirty-five
Flight Ten, Darwin to Cairns

After another appalling night's sleep, courtesy of the alien, and rudely awoken by a 04.00 alarm call, it was not the best way to start the day. At the airport, they found a blue flame lighter buried in the depths of my handbag, which I didn't even realize, was there, and they confiscated it. It was a bit of a shame as it was a fun novelty lighter I had bought in Spain from a deaf and dumb man. I couldn't help but wonder what they would do with my lovely lighter with the big red flashing boobies. Keep it probably. This was slightly ironic having already gotten through several customs officials undetected; certainly makes you wonder about airport security.

Today we flew to Cairns in order to go to Port Douglas. We arrived in Port Douglas at 10.00, which to us seemed much later, unsurprisingly. We made a conscious decision not to stay in Cairns but to drive a little further out to Port Douglas to visit a small family-run boutique hotel situated on a four-mile beach. We were shown to our room, which was just beautiful, and it was a most glorious day. We had a proper ocean view room where I just sat and gazed out to sea; this was definitely the best room we've had so far in Australia.

Rather strangely, I was intensely aware that not for the first time I actually felt at peace with myself. Why in the world did I feel this way? Was it spiritual? I really

My Travels with Wheely

didn't know. At this precise moment, I was in seventh heaven. This was where I wanted to be forever. We had our own sitting room and it was now that I wanted to invite friends over for a drink, but I couldn't; they weren't here.

We decided to go for a walk by the sea, and David managed to get me as close as he could. I was so near and so excited. I could feel the spray on my face and almost touch the water. I tried so hard but couldn't. This was a truly beautiful place with all the right ingredients for making it somewhere you never wanted to leave. The smell of the fresh sea air was one that I wanted to bottle and keep forever, if only I could.

Then we ventured into the town not far from the hotel, which was full of life, and for a small place it had a lot more going on here than in Darwin. There was a fabulous market, and we bought fruit, ham, cheese, and bread for supper tonight and the obligatory bottle of wine. We liked being here and felt at home immediately. Port Douglas was so stunning.

We enjoyed the most perfect evening on our balcony, as the sound of the sea gently lapped in the background, and we ate our food and drank our wine feeling very happy indeed.

E-mails Received

Dear DallAwayDays, Thanks for very newsy e-mail. This book you're writing will be a bestseller! Love your description of the attractiveness of the Abos. Thanks for sharing your experiences. C&NB

Nicky Dalladay

Shameful to say that I did forget your birthday, so belated wishes to you, my dear! What a great way to spend your birthday. Thank you so much for your running commentary, it brightens up my otherwise quite dull existence. Keep them coming. MP

Did my eyes deceive me; did somebody just mention the word book?

Day Thirty-six

Sat on the balcony, I was enjoying the air and view, but without warning the bubble burst. I felt very melancholy today, and it was at times like this I wanted the impossible: to be able to walk. The reality was I always wished I could still walk, that feeling doesn't ever leave me, but never more so than right now. Why now? I am at my happiest by the sea, and I wished with all my heart I could run over there and get into the sea and feel the warmth of the sand underfoot, but I couldn't and that's all there was to it.

I was increasingly aware of the amount of effort David has had to go through, and I felt so utterly helpless and completely useless being unable to assist him. I had to watch him run around and do everything while I could do nothing; it was not a great feeling. We are husband and wife, but because of my physical disabilities it has made me feel that I can no longer contribute to our relationship. My guess is that a lot of people won't understand what I mean. Yes my head and heart still work, but it is not enough for me. The core of my soul has been stolen from me; I am no longer the person I was once. I have to say I couldn't believe my luck to have met such an amazing man, and what a wonderful bright shining star to have in my life. I am indeed a very lucky woman.

Anyway, as they say, the show must go on.

It was now six weeks since we had left home, and

Nicky Dalladay

Bangkok and Vietnam seemed like a lifetime ago. Luckily we would have our pictures to remind us just how it was. We now thought about where we were in terms of our itinerary as we were on the last leg of our Australian visit. If anyone were to ask what our favourite destination was in this sector, it would have been Sydney, which was fantastic. That was, until we arrived in Port Douglas, which was equally fantastic. They were very different from each other in numerous ways, and both were pretty special.

Today was another day spent billing and cooing over this place; it had to be paradise. Although I do recall saying the exact same thing about Bermuda some thirty years ago, but that was then and this was now, with David. There was a beautiful little church right by the sea, and David was dispatched to go in and take some photographs so I could see for myself what it was like. It was just so stunning. There was an open window behind the altar that looked straight out to the sea, creating a moving picture; it was utterly breathtaking. We noted that they performed all ceremonies here, apart from funerals, which I was guessing was because it was not necessarily a good selling point. Having said that, you don't necessarily have to sell death, it is something that will happen to everyone in due course. We instantly decided that we would like to spend the rest of our days here, and once again we pinched ourselves.

At about 16.00, I thought that today was our wedding anniversary, and we reckoned we'd been married for eighteen years, but neither of us knew off the top of our heads. We could of course work it out, but that seemed rather insignificant, and we felt as though we had been together forever. The beauty of being comfortable with

My Travels with Wheely

each other was more than enough. We didn't do presents anymore since we had all that we needed: each other.

It was such a shame that I couldn't record the smell of the sea and the plants, because it was sublime. Pictures are able to jog your memory, but there was nothing to capture the smell. The plants here were just enormous, as you'd expect in the tropics really. It certainly made nonsense of our little potted plants at home.

E-mails Received

We have just been catching up with your latest adventures, and it is good to read you are having such a fantastic time. Sorry to hear about Wheely; hope it isn't terminal, perhaps a change of bandages every few days will help it get through its journey. Happy Anniversary. M&A

If you are reading this, you were not eaten by: cannibals (Torres Straight is notorious for that) sharks, or salties (crocodiles). I hope you avoided yellow fever, malaria, Ross river fever, sand fly bites, stone fish and jellyfish stings to name but a few of the hazards of the tropical North. In spite of the very real hazards up there it can be a very beautiful place. NZ will be very peaceful and the people are friendly. The Maoris are nothing like our Aborigines. We hope the rest of your adventure is happy and healthy. It was a pleasure to meet such good poms on the Ghan. M&P

Thanks for the entertaining update on your travels in Aus. Sounds like you're enjoying Aus a lot, knew you would, despite the aborigines/flies etc. My daughter spent a week in Alice working there, and she actually did

Nicky Dalladay

see the river in flood, it was a major event and everyone downed tools to go and see, apparently if you see the river in flood three times you are considered a local. Sorry I missed your birthday; no one tells me anything! But glad you had a good one, how could you not when on a fantastic trip? Everything very quiet here, no significant news apart from a dead swan in France, which had avian flu, but given where you have been, that's a bit of a none story for you! Hope Wheely continues to make a full recovery. JRB

A note to wish Nicky a belated happy birthday; it sounds like you had such a lovely day. I loved reading your e-mail, so pleased to hear that you are having such a fantastic time, sorry to hear about Wheely. Look forward to your next missive. GH

Sorry not to have sent you a birthday e-mail, but there was no access to the computer. Glad you celebrated in style; I was thinking of you on the day. Delighted you're having a great time still and hope that Wheely gets you through the rest of your trip. DJ

Shame on me that I didn't send a birthday e-mail; I was a little bit stressed out with my IMC exam. Glad you are having such a fantastic time! I'm so jealous but you deserve this wonderful trip and the experience with it. Your trip notes sound so exciting, always looking forward to getting the next update. Back here in London nothing exciting happens. Weather wise we cannot compete with the sunshine you experience at the moment. It is grey and windy here today. PW

My Travels with Wheely

Sounds like you're having a lovely time. I am waiting at Stansted Airport to fly to Cornwall, got to go hope all is well. KM

More messages from home. Yes, we were correct; it had been our wedding anniversary. Yet more weather reports and confirmation about the river Adelaide.

Day Thirty-seven
Third Helicopter Flight

What a wonderful day we had. We went on Motorcycle Trike tour. It was quoted as "a stimulating way to see our piece of paradise. So forget the crowds, tinted glass, and air conditioning, chuck on your sunnies, jump on the scoot, get some wind in your face, and we'll show you the only way to tour." The Australians do have a unique way of putting things. We were picked up by somebody who introduced himself as Chief, wearing his black leathers, and he was sat on the most magnificent Red Trike.

Up into the mountains we felt the fresh coolness of the air, down again through the rain, and then to feel the warmth of the brilliant sunshine, he took us everywhere. Chief was a wonderful companion, and we stopped to have a cup of coffee with him where we were introduced to some of the motorbike fraternity. They all had the look of ageing hippies and had weather-beaten skin.

It was an amazing day and a beautiful experience on this mighty machine. It didn't matter that my legs didn't work; I felt as free as a butterfly — so much so that words failed me.

The morning was truly brilliant, but then the afternoon was still to come with yet more fun. We had booked another helicopter flight, this being our third of the trip.

My Travels with Wheely

Where this time? We were scheduled to have a scenic rainforest and reef flight, as well as the Great Barrier Reef, an awesome sight which can apparently be seen from the moon — not that I'd know that, having never been to the moon. This was indeed another moment where we needed to pinch ourselves, and by now we must surely be covered with bruises, a small price to pay. This was such a magnificent sight and the colour changes in the water were something rather special: deep blue and a bright turquoise, and the sand caves just seemed to lie on the water.

Adam was our pilot for the expedition, and I asked him if he loved his job as he was very lucky to get to see this every day, but he said he didn't really think about it too much. I supposed for him the novelty had worn off. Prior to becoming a pilot, he was in the circus as a trapeze artist whilst his brother, also in the circus, was a lion tamer. His father was a clown doing children's parties, which was what Adam was now going to go into, because, unbelievably, you could earn far more money doing that than being a pilot.

He commended us on our travelling and not just sitting about doing nothing. Life offered you many choices, but it was up to you which route you took. His mum was disabled and hadn't left the house for nine years, and she had withdrawn so much that she'd given up on life; he was going to tell her about me.

After the flight, David divulged that he'd felt nauseous as the helicopter was banking a fair bit and dropping. I felt my tummy go over a little but was okay; to me it was

Nicky Dalladay

a bit like a fairground ride. Not to worry, a good old cup of tea would sort him out.

We fully appreciated we were immensely privileged to be doing what we were doing, and I couldn't help but feel very emotional about it.

E-mail Received

It sounds as if you are having a wonderful time and telling a great story! EM

We were having an absolutely fantastic time. We were, as they say, "Living the dream."

My Travels with Wheely

The Magnificent Red Trike

Day Thirty-eight

We were now on our last few days of our time in Australia. This leg of the journey was drawing to a close, but we decided not to dwell on it. Today we were going on another boat trip to go snorkelling in the Great Barrier Reef; it was hardly an exclusive trip since we would be accompanied by several hundred people all doing the same.

We got to the reef in a couple of hours and made our way to the diving platform. We changed into our not-so-flattering purple diving suits, and Starbucks cappuccinos, cookies, and muffins were evident for all to see. I had a few reservations about this particular trip, like how I was actually going to get in, and then once in, and how on Earth I would manoeuvre in the water. All these questions and all I wanted to see were the fish and coral.

I was suddenly full of fear. The platform was equipped with a special chair to lower me into the water, although it was but a humble white plastic garden chair. A guide took great care of me and gently helped me into the water. Sadly, I then encountered some sort of panic attack and suddenly felt very vulnerable and unable to cope. A really lovely chap spent time giving me some confidence and took me out to where I would be able to see some of the reef; this was indeed a very special moment he had given me.

My Travels with Wheely

The reef was beautiful, but not as striking as I'd been led to believe. I thought there were a number of reasons for this; perhaps the reef itself had suffered from so many tourist visits, and we had just managed to increase that. It was also a very cloudy day, and the beauty would be enhanced by brilliant sunshine. Lastly I thought you really needed to be much further out to see just how tremendous it was. Before we knew it, we were back on the boat and the weather was beginning to close in even more. David was taking a few pictures and suddenly the camera made an extraordinary noise, stopped working, and gave up completely. Damn and blast; what were we going to do now?

Back at Port Douglas we went out for dinner and enjoyed looking at the sea and listening to the sound of the gentle lapping of the waves; it was perfect. After dinner we took a stroll by the sea and spent our penultimate night in Australia gazing at the stars.

Day Thirty-nine

This was our last full day here, and we got to see another tropical rainstorm. Wow, this was fantastic and so warm; this really was the wet season, no doubt about that. First thing in the morning we read through our insurance policy and noted we had to go the police station and report that our camera was broken, which we duly did. For the life of me I couldn't understand why it was necessary to go to the police station. What would they say? As it turned out, unsurprisingly, they were not in the least bit interested for the moment; we would have to put this issue on the back burner and deal with it when we got home.

The torrential rain hardly stopped all day, and the only time it did was when we were in the car; typical. We were on a trip to go up into the mountains and rainforest, which entailed travelling in a cable car. Mighty strange to be in a cable car where the land all around you was a brilliant green, as we were used to this mode of transport when we used to go skiing. The rainforest was incredible, and we marvelled at the size of the plants and just how lush it all was, and it was still pouring.

The cable car station took us to a place called Karunda, which was a small town that had been set up for tourists, so as you'd expect, it was a little tacky. We had to spend half an hour there before we could catch the 15.30 train back down the mountain; it was then that this funny

My Travels with Wheely

little place shut down completely. The train journey was lovely and we enjoyed the spectacular scenery in the rain as we wound our way down.

Glen, our driver, was at the bottom ready to meet us and take us on to Cairns for an hour. He dropped everyone else off at a convenient point before taking us to the only camera shop within several hundred miles. The camera shop looked at the ailing camera and announced there was nothing they could do, so the only option was to purchase another one. Drenched through, clutching our sick camera and our new one, we headed for home.

Tonight we dined on good old Oz fair: kangaroo for me and barramundi for David. We have had the most amazing time in Australia and firmly believed that we had saved the best of it until last.

Day Forty
Flight Eleven, Cairns to Auckland

We left the wonderful Port Douglas and suddenly realized we had not heard the sound of constantly clicking cameras, and the Japanese were not around. We arrived at the airport only to discover the three million, or thereabouts, Japanese tourists were all in the queue for customs. Perhaps I could appear in more photographs, although somehow I doubted this. Mrs. Bossy Boots (me) decided I wasn't having any of that and sent David off to seek out an official, which he duly did. Hey presto, we managed to bypass the enormous queue to go straight to the front.

Now I haven't dwelled on the customs officials yet, so I might take this opportunity to do so. They are indeed a very odd bunch of people who seemed to be rather lacking in humour or have had a personality bypass. We got to the point where David had to put our ever-growing hand luggage through the x-ray machine, empty the contents of his pockets, and remove his belt and shoes before he could walk through the barriers. I, on the other hand, got shoved to one side and then was asked if I can walk. What was it with these people? Do those who sit in wheelchairs normally walk? Had I perhaps missed something? Obviously, the answer was a polite no, whilst my head had its own thoughts.

My Travels with Wheely

When I watched this surly woman put on her rubber gloves and thought to myself, *my god what on earth did she intend to do?* She "Ms Surly" then proceeded to inform me what she was about to do, basically feel me all over, inspect every little bit of Wheely she could and, by the way, " did I understand". Of course, I understood, I wasn't that stupid. She then set about the task in hand and did the thing she was employed to do. I didn't enjoy being manhandled in this manner, I realized however that certain jobs must be done; I just think they could be done with a little more humour.

It was my mission in life to get a smile from some of the most miserable people I encountered. Suffice it to say I managed to get her smiling by the end. It was at that moment that I decided that going forward, I'd give the people who searched me — but only if it was a memorable experience — a score out of ten. Ms. Surly would be awarded with a five and serve as my benchmark. We survived the customs ordeal and headed for the business-class lounge to get the next e-mail update sent.

Fifth E-mail

I stupidly forgot to mention something important about Darwin. On our last day we went to the aviation centre and saw one of the two B-52s outside of the USA. Well, my dears, what can I say, but David was simply beside himself with joy. I on the other hand took it completely in stride and duly waited outside in the sunshine. I did ask the man where the other B-52 was and was told "a little place called Duxford," just twenty minutes up the road from us at home. Just as well we haven't travelled

Nicky Dalladay

around the world to see this thing.

In Vietnam I purchased a traditional Vietnamese hat, which at the time was a necessity, and we have carried it around on our travels. Now, bearing in mind our luggage is already full to bursting, we decided the time had come for something to go. It was a bit of a toss-up, I can tell you, between "Freddy frame" and my Vietnamese hat, and in the end I chose to ditch the hat, after all; I didn't have to carry Freddy. Anyway, we dumped my stylish hat at the local branch of the Red Cross in downtown Darwin. Well, you can imagine my sheer delight, which I showed more for the hat than the aforementioned B-52 (sorry, David), when one of the local aborigines was sat in the sun swilling his beer and smoking a cigarette, looking very cool in what had been my hat. I'm thrilled it went to a good home.

Anyway, back to where we are now, Port Douglas. We had never seen anywhere quite so beautiful. It renders you speechless, and there are insufficient words to describe it. Suffice it to say, David and I have decided it's where we would like to spend the rest of our days. There is the most beautiful church right by the sea called St. Mary's By the Sea, no less.

We achieved so much in PD and a few of them are mentioned: a helicopter flight over the GBR and the rainforest. We went up into the mountains on a motorcycle, and that trip was brilliant. A boat trip to the GBR to snorkel, a cable car and scenic train ride (the last two happened in a tropical storm; now we really know why it's called the wet season!). We loved being in PD

My Travels with Wheely

and say we saved the best of Oz until last.

We are currently at the airport waiting for our flight to take us to NZ.

We realize we've been away for quite a while when we have to replenish things like toothpaste and deodorant. We are having a ball and meeting some fabulous people on the way.

I don't know if anyone has sent text messages because we were recently told of one that was sent to us, but we didn't receive it. If anyone sends a message, we always respond, so if you haven't had a reply from a text please, resend it.

Love to everyone
The DallAwayDays
xxxx

Nicky Dalladay

Well, we eventually boarded the plane and sat in comfort whilst we sipped our champagne. How decadent we felt once again. The journey was not too bad, the alien had behaved quite well, and we arrived in Auckland some hours later in the middle of the evening. I didn't know why, well I did really, but instead of just getting a taxi straight to the hotel we opted for the shuttle bus. We suddenly decided to watch our pennies as we were, after all, about to deviate from our normal way of life and travel independently. There was a drawback as we hadn't considered the length of time the shuttle was going to take. I could safely say that on reflection, it was a really stupid idea.

The driver so loved the sound of his own voice that you'd think he was some sort of tour guide. He pointed out everything there was to possibly mention, and we just wanted to get to the hotel. By the time we arrived, it was late evening. The hotel was just stunning. What a great shame we were not going to get any time to spend in it. On the walls hung pictures of noteworthy dignitaries and an archive of famous actors who stayed there. We were so very sorry not to have booked a couple of nights in Auckland, and I wasn't quite sure why we hadn't; again, hindsight was such a wonderful thing.

We were shown to our bedroom, which was fabulous, and rather than doing the most sensible thing and going to bed, we went to the bar to have a swift beer instead. Beside the bar was a terrific cigar room with a very extensive range of cigars that could only have been described as a cigar smoker's paradise. The drawback being, of course, that since the introduction of the world

My Travels with Wheely

smoking ban, you couldn't smoke your cigar in the cigar lounge. If you wished to imbibe in the filthy habit of smoking you were invited to go outside and stand on the pavement, so suddenly the appeal vanished for David.

Day Forty-one

Early in the morning we took a taxi back to the airport. If only we had given this just a little more thought, we should have stayed at the airport hotel on the previous night. Not for the first time, we had made a mistake. Today was the day we were to go and pick up our two-berth deluxe campervan. We were both so excited about the prospect of travelling around this country in a campervan and considered this was the only way it should be done. It really was going to be back to basics for us. No more hotels for the next twenty days or so; the thought of travelling around the country footloose and fancy free was most appealing.

Goodness, the campervan was quite a big thing, very long, but once all of our luggage, the walking frame, and Wheely were stowed, it was absolutely packed out. We made a stop to stock up with provisions, and we made tracks and zoomed off on our adventure. Only we didn't zoom anywhere, we crawled along; they had the most ridiculous speed restriction of 20mph.

We had a very rough plan of where we thought we wanted to go, but it was always going to be a moveable feast, so we headed in the direction of Waihi Beach. It was a glorious day and whilst the sun was shining it had a very fresh feel about it, and as we had both anticipated, the scenery was beautiful. We couldn't find the campsite that David had earmarked for us to stay in but happened on the

My Travels with Wheely

Bowen campsite. It was nestled between the sea and a lake and was a gorgeous setting. We found ourselves checking in. This was a new experience for us, and we found it quite exciting.

Suddenly, we found ourselves having to make choices: would we like a non-powered site or a powered one? We figured that having power was probably quite important so we paid for a powered site. Now we found ourselves in very unfamiliar territory and needed to work out just what had to be done to get us up and running. I imagined any onlookers were laughing at us, not unkindly I hasten to add, just probably thinking that clearly we were new to this. Couldn't say I blamed them, really; after all, we were. After deliberating about what went where we were set and ready to go — not literally, you understand, just metaphorically.

Fortunately, we had decided just after picking up the campervan to go and get some food, and it suddenly occurred to us that we had not passed a single shop on the way. Come to think of it, we hadn't passed any restaurants or for that matter another living soul. Without further ado, David started preparing our supper.

It was so wonderful not to be in a hotel. They could be so restrictive, and I didn't think they were really suited to our new life on the road. It made a really nice change, and we just sat, ate, and chatted. Later on, David wrestled with making the bed up, which meant converting the dining area into a sleeping one, which was quite clever really. So, time for bed, we crawled in via the foot end, and I had to move like some sort of slug to get in properly.

Nicky Dalladay

It was jolly cold in the campervan, and we could see our breath. The pillows were covered in some sort of plastic that crackled every time you moved, just like the pillows in hospital. Oh, this was horrible; I didn't like this very much. Where did the happy hippy travellers go? I wondered. Not even one night had passed and we were already missing our creature comforts, especially a comfortable bed. In order to take my mind off this situation, I found myself gazing out the window and looking at the stars. I was awestruck by the magnitude of the beauty I was looking at, and for the reward of such a sight I instantly decided it was most definitely worth a small amount of discomfort; it was out of this world.

E-mails Received

Lovely getting your update just before we go to France skiing tomorrow. The rainforest from a helicopter sounds particularly spectacular. Sounds like you're having an absolutely wonderful time. C&NB

Delighted to hear things are going well. Port Douglas is obviously worth a visit. Trust David has now got over the excitement of the B-52, although possibly not. Sounds like there are an awful lot of abos sitting around in the streets drinking, civilized society. Pleased to hear your hat went to a good cause, no doubt keeping the beer cold in the shade prior to consumption. RA

I do hope you took a picture of the aborigine in your hat. DJ

We simply *love* to read your e-mails. They are a wonderful read so please keep them coming. GD

My Travels with Wheely

I am finding your e-mails really interesting, and I think that you express the same sentiments as us in regards to Alice Springs, etc. We have been to Port Douglas and also found it beautiful as well, but I just hope you can get to beaches here in NZ as I am sure you will find somewhere just as nice. D from TLG

More messages. Strangely no weather reports this time. Have the Brits tired of informing us about the lousy temperatures?

Day Forty-two

Up bright and breezy we departed the campsite and went to the bay to take some photos before heading for Rotorua for a two-night stop. Having spent most of the day travelling and taking in the wonderful scenery, we found a campsite next to the Blue Lake, which was one of the many hundreds of lakes in New Zealand. The setting was idyllic, and we gasped at the beauty. I felt New Zealand was not going to be the least bit disappointing.

Given the key to the disabled toilets to retain for our stay, we felt rather pleased that we didn't have to shower with the masses, although there actually weren't that many people around as it was the end of the season. We ventured forth to the disabled facilities, and it amused me somewhat, that disabled people apparently didn't seem to want to wash their hands afterward as there wasn't soap nor paper towels, both of which were supplied in the able-bodied toilets. For a few minutes I pondered over this. Had I been discriminated against? I thought not, they had probably just forgotten them.

Supper was enjoyed with a lovely bottle of wine, and David set about making the bed up again for the night. It was so peaceful here it was wonderful, and we spent another night just gazing at the stars. It was captivating, and I felt sure that it was the Milky Way I was looking at, but of course I had absolutely no idea.

My Travels with Wheely

E-mail Received

Hi to the Travelling Dalladays, Love your postcards from the dark side of the Earth. Although…not for C, who's in a state of panic just reading about it being far too hot, and you must promise not to tell her about Vietnam when you return. Anyway, glad to hear you're having such a wonderful trip. Sorry you missed the snow here. P &CF

Someone needs to toughen up.

Day Forty-three

Not an early start; well, there's a surprise. You could almost accuse us of only having two speeds: very slow or stop. Today we went to Waimangu Volcanic Valley for a walking tour and a boat trip. The walking tour took us along the crater walkways where we saw the awe-inspiring volcanic activity and thermally adapted plants. During our walk our nostrils were filled with the very unpleasant aroma of sulphur. If you just so happen to like the smell of bad eggs, all well and good, if you didn't, unlucky. Frying Pan Lake is the world's largest hot water spring, and it was quite fascinating to see the water bubbling, as the nearest I had ever come to seeing something boiling was in a saucepan on the stove. It was quite incredible to see the volcanic activity in the water and the steam rising.

We made our way back to the campsite for what would no doubt be another cold night on the now permanently called "bus." It would be easy to interpret this as being miserable about it, which was most definitely not the case; the problem was solved with just a few more layers of clothing. I reminded myself that this part of the campervan experience was my idea, and I still maintained that whilst I didn't particularly like the sleeping conditions, I very much liked the freedom of our bus.

New Zealand was pretty much how we expected it

My Travels with Wheely

to be, which was extraordinarily beautiful. We hadn't really travelled far through it yet, though the parts we had seen were so lush, and with the size of the vegetation you would be forgiven for thinking you were in the tropics. However, it was much colder here than we had anticipated, and although it was the end of their summer, we didn't really have the right clothes with us. Who was it who thought she had packed enough to cover every eventuality?

Travelling along the road in our bus made me us feel as though we should turn into hippies, wear caftans, and smoke a little dope, but naturally we were not doing any of those things, although my hair had grown a little longer, but that was about it. We were as scruffy as scruffy could be, but we just didn't care. We were cool with everything and absolutely loved the freedom that came with being on the open road. In fact, we were so chilled out that we were virtually horizontal. More importantly we were, at that moment, very happy with life. I decided that a temporary name change was in order, and for the duration of New Zealand, we would become "Mr. & Mrs. Moonshine."

I feel that I should just touch on the sheep myth; we didn't see that many, certainly not the quantities we joked about at home, so I'd like to put the kibosh on that one. Granted, there were an awful lot of cows to be seen, but who knows? Perhaps the sheep would be more evident the further South we travelled.

Day Forty-four

The bus and all of its passengers left Roturua and made its way to Napier. En route, we stopped at Lake Taupo, which is the largest lake in New Zealand and is oh so very beautiful. It is made even more so with the sun out, although it was chilly. Typical, the British have to make some comment about the weather. David parked the bus and we stopped for a bite to eat. That was the great benefit of having all you needed on board — you just stopped wherever you fancied.

We continued our drive to Napier, and we only seemed to pass through green, lush, and beautiful scenery. Isn't there anything here that's ugly?

Checked in at the campsite in Napier, decided to splash out for two nights, and we opted for a self-contained unit — what luxury! — all things being relative when compared to the bus. At least David would be spared from having to assemble the bed and dismantle it in the morning; it should be a bit of rest for him. Having said it should be a bit of a rest for him, I now find that he's gone in search of the laundry; the washing had started to mount up, my heart went out to him once more, and there had not been one single complaint from him.

Today, whilst the alien had not returned, it was instead the turn of the "drain" that had the unenviable responsibility of draining all the life out of me. I was left more physically

My Travels with Wheely

useless than I was the day before. The drain had managed to single-handedly deprive me of any physical ability, and no amount of coaxing and swearing at my legs would get them to move. Getting on and off the bus was more difficult than ever; how I hated this cruel condition. I really didn't want to exist like this, and my demeanour was deflated. Today was yet another day that I would have to wrestle with my emotions and dig deep within myself. In the past I have thought about which situation I hated most of all — the alien or the drain? Both were equally as bad as each other, so it could never be a contest.

David could only observe what my body was going through and was only able to comfort me in the way that somebody who loves you could, whilst I continued to cry on his shoulder.

E-mails Received

I love your e-mails. They are so full of enthusiasm and excitement; I admire you both so much and wish I was there too. I had not checked my e-mails for about a week or so and your last two had arrived, so I printed them off and read them like a chapter from a book; it was great. I can tell you are having a ball and I am so pleased for you both. I look forward to your next instalments. SW

Your messages are without a doubt the best of the day. By far the nicest and most interesting e-mails…Nicky, I dearly hope you will start putting a book together and continue to write, as you really have got the skills, they should really not be wasted. I love the duct tape, and the poor Wheely part is fantastic. Thinking of the two of you

Nicky Dalladay

and wishing you a continuous beautiful time, and Nicky, please do think of writing this book. It would be funny, enlightening, and very interesting. MK

We don't really expect to hear from you during this time as we see you will now be travelling all around New Zealand in your campervan. So we expect a long e-mail on this part of the trip…can't wait. S could relate to a lot of what you said about Oz and can really understand how you feel about Port Douglas. He told us that he drove through a number of abo towns in the Outback and very much agrees with your comments they must have been last in the line when the Lord created man and woman! S said they were basically okay. He would not contemplate bringing one home to mum. I am interested if you find New Zealand slower, gentler, and greener… and how many sheep did you manage to count? GD

The dreaded word *book* has been mentioned again. Did they really mean it and should I act upon it? I would seriously have to think about that one.

Day Forty-five

Last night the drain seemed to take mercy on me, and my disposition today had returned to normality, thankfully. The accommodation in Napier was basic but clean and tidy; the main thing being it was more comfortable than the bus. What had happened to Mr. & Mrs. Moonshine? They seemed to have gone a little soft; had their great British spirit been left firmly on their bus?

The previous night we had booked to go on a wine tour today, to go to Hawke's Bay to visit six wineries, and we were supposed to be picked up at 10.30. When we were still waiting twenty minutes later, David went to call them to see what the delay was. Evidently, they had actually forgotten about us. The woman who owned the company came to get us with her tail between her legs; it was her fault. No matter, she took us to the first winery, and we picked up the tour. Grant was our tour guide for the day; he was lovely and a very amusing man who certainly knew about wine. Needless to say, after visiting six drinking establishments, we arrived back at the campsite a little worse for wear. It could even be said we were somewhat tipsy, but it had been a jolly good day.

Day Forty-six

We deviated from the rough plan we had made in order to go to Martinborough, and we popped over to the west side of the country. We were getting nearer and nearer to Wellington and kept stopping to look at campsites, but they were either too grim or they were full. We were a little taken aback as it was supposed to be the end of the season. No problem; we would just have to keep driving. It was taking so long to find anywhere that we both got pretty fed up. We were tired and hungry and seemingly unable to talk because of our frustration. I supposed it was at that moment that I suspected neither of us was really cut out for becoming full-time hippy travellers. What a shame.

A change of tactics was required, and we decided to look for motels, since there was obviously something big going on in Wellington, resulting in the serious lack of availability. Eventually we found a motel with a free room, largely due to the helpful people en route. Apart from thinking you had stepped back into the dubious decor of the 1950s, it was certainly big enough to house several families, so the donkey train should fit in quite nicely. Oh, it was grim to look at, but at least it was clean.

Having spent so much time trying to find somewhere to stay for the night we had in fact covered a lot more distance than we originally wanted. So much so we were

My Travels with Wheely

a day ahead of ourselves.

To cross from the North Island to the South Island you needed to take a ferry, which we had previously booked in the United Kingdom for 4 March. David proceeded to call the ferry office and changed our crossing to the Third. This was not a particularly good move, as we were yet to discover.

Day Forty-seven

We drove to the ferry terminal and were several hours too early for our 14.30 crossing; you may recall that I mentioned earlier that David liked to arrive everywhere in good time. In fact, the 10.00 ferry had not yet left and was running late due to adverse weather conditions, which didn't bode well. However, we were on the waitlist for going on last, but then it occurred to David that he hadn't told them I was disabled. It transpired that because I was in a wheelchair, it would be necessary for us to board the ferry first for the simple reason that we would be by the lift. We sat on the bus and watched the delayed ferry commence its journey to the South Island. It actually left forty-five minutes later than it was scheduled to leave, and we would have to sit at the front of the queue for several hours and just wait patiently for the next one. We noticed that the water was quite rough and vaguely wondered just how good our sea legs would be.

Right now, I felt the need to record a note whilst David was not in earshot; he has just popped out for a coffee and a sandwich. I can't express just how indebted I am to him. None of this trip would have been possible by myself; I just couldn't contemplate it, but it was just as well I would never think of doing it alone. What an amazing man he is, constantly rendering me speechless; how lucky am I to have him in my life. I often chastise myself with how angry and frustrated I get but must

My Travels with Wheely

remember that he also goes through the same emotions I do. We are in this together. It is not just me who has MS; he suffers as well by having to deal with me. He is quite simply one of life's unsung heroes. I was slightly emotional at this point but am glad I have taken time to say this.

Eventually, we boarded the ferry and were, as promised, loaded first directly behind the trucks, just so I could be near the lift for easy access. Upstairs we made our way to the passenger deck and noted the large piles of sick bags being put out. Blimey, what were they expecting? It was a nice day, although a touch windy. Anyway, we made our way outside, as that was where we preferred to be, out in the fresh air and enjoying the scenery. The ferry started to move and our journey was underway with a travel time of three hours predicted. We felt sure the time would go quickly. Just half an hour in and the waves changed; they were much bigger than before, although the skies were still pleasant. The roll of the ferry got greater and there was noticeable activity by the crew. I wouldn't say they were panicking, but there was definitely something afoot. They announced that the dining room was going to be shut until further notice; oh, I didn't like the sound of this.

Still outside and chatting with fellow passengers we were enjoying the crossing, albeit a little rough. A lady by the name of Heather-Jane introduced herself, and we had great fun talking, laughing, and looking at the sea in awe. Meanwhile, her fiancé, Nick, was inside, apparently looking a little green and feeling very seasick and last seen clutching a sick bag in readiness.

Nicky Dalladay

By now, we were more than four hours into our journey and still had the North Island very much in our sights; so much for the three hours. A young girl who had previously been outside with us came rushing out and said, "You do not want to go in there; the smell is just awful." By all accounts, the pile of sick bags was reducing rapidly with demand outstripping supply; it was for this reason that I opted to remain outside even though it was getting quite chilly.

Heather-Jane told me how she and Nick met, and it was a beautiful love story. They were both nineteen and living in the United Kingdom when they got engaged. However, the engagement was called off for the simple reason they both felt they were far too young to make such as huge commitment. They both went their separate ways, he to Australia and her to Sussex, both entered into marriages some years later, and subsequently, they lost touch. Now in their forties and both divorced, they found each other and took up from where they left off. They were so in love with one another, it was romantic and beautiful, and I imagined a Mills & Boon story in the making.

Whilst she relayed this story we had not really taken much notice of the pitching and rolling of the ferry, until Wheely and I suddenly careered into the railings on the side of the boat. David and Heather-Jane threw themselves toward Wheely, managing to grab the wheels. The three of us came face-to-face with the sea; we were so near we felt the spray of the water in our faces. With the help of others we managed to get to safety, and we all just laughed. This was indeed an extremely dramatic incident; realistically, it could easily have turned into a disaster.

My Travels with Wheely

When I was facing the sea and was so very near it, I remained very calm with death staring me in the face. I wasn't frightened, I just felt that if it was my time, then so be it. In a way, if I'm being totally honest, I saw it as a possible way out. My deteriorating body would no longer be a problem, and I would grieve no more. Every time part of my body changes and loses the ability to function properly, I liken it to a form of bereavement. I have to go through a grieving process and get used to the way my body now works. I am guilty sometimes of embellishing the truth so as to make a story sound a little more interesting, but this experience is straight from my heart, the truth.

It was obviously not my destiny to end my days this way, and it was then you start to think of all the sea disaster movies you have ever seen, and the *Titanic* flashes through your mind. We all know the outcome of that.

We had originally set sail in an eight metre swell, but this had now been exceeded and was way over twelve metres. It was actually quite incredible to witness, and the sea commands and deserves a huge amount of respect. This was a truly very rough crossing with about 95 percent of the passengers "chucking up"; this was my worst nightmare coming true, vomit that is, and it wasn't even over yet.

The captain had made the decision to turn the boat in the hope that he could find some calmer waters, much to the relief of the 95 percent of the passengers who were ailing big time. In order to execute this though, we needed to be inside the boat. Damn…I would have to endure the smell of puke, and that was so not fair. We were informed to brace ourselves and told it was likely to

Nicky Dalladay

be bad. Great, more good news.

In all honesty it wasn't that bad, and no sooner had the turn been made you could feel the calmness of the water. We knew it was better when we heard the announcement that the dining room would reopen shortly and we would be provided with a free sandwich and a drink. Later on, we would also be receiving complimentary fish and chips. This turned out to be a fantastic trip. We had experienced an awful lot of excitement and free food, and as if that wasn't enough, we were told that someone would be coming around to see us to arrange for a full refund of our ferry crossing cost. It was so brilliant that I would have been inclined to pay them more for the privilege. Even if you had wanted to, you would never have been able to plan any of this.

At roughly 22.30 the ferry docked, and by 22.45 the foot passengers were told they could disembark. By this time, it felt like the new friends you'd met at the beginning of the journey were now old mates. Meanwhile, all other passengers were asked to remain seated until further notice as there was extensive damage in the hold. It would appear that the severe roll we had encountered — you know, the bit where Wheely and I made a dash for the railings — was enough to turn the trucks on their side and send them crashing into the campervans. The campervans had crashed into each other and had rolled forward into the cars. They began to call out the registration numbers of the damaged vehicles, and this went on for what seemed like an eternity as we waited patiently for ours to be called out, but it wasn't.

My Travels with Wheely

By some miracle our campervan had not been mentioned. At 23.30 those registration numbers that were not called out were allowed to return to their vehicles in order to disembark. Well, when we got into the hold we saw the utter devastation. It was complete carnage. We were sure it would have been worse on first sight, but it was awful for those poor people who had temporarily had their lives ruined. We really had to count our blessings, you know, because if I hadn't been disabled we would have met the same fate. But if I hadn't been disabled we wouldn't even be on the trip of a lifetime in the first place, it's as simple as that.

Finally and with much relief we arrived at Picton campsite not far from the ferry and drove into a powered site for the night. Well, beggars can't be choosers, can they?

We got into bed, but it was a very restless night and neither of us could sleep. We could only think of the events of that day. A lot of people had their holidays ruined, and we felt sorry for them; we had managed to come away completely unscathed.

Day Forty-eight

Woke up in the morning and discovered we were the talk of the campsite. There was another couple who had also shared the same journey. People were coming up to us and saying, "My goodness, we hear you were on that crossing and it was quite an awful journey." When you stopped to think about it, yes it was, but at the time it seemed nothing.

The realization began to sink in during the course of the day, and we both began to feel quite sick, but we put it down to the aftershock of what had happened. There were a few injuries sustained but nothing major. We were all so lucky to be able to walk off, or rather wheel off in my case, from the boat.

The timing of our day was now completely in array. We left the campsite later than anticipated heading for Kaikoura, but en route we stopped at a winery — to be more specific, not just any winery but Marlborough's Montana Brancott Winery. Montana is a great favourite of ours, so we treated ourselves to a wine tasting and a spot of lunch there, which was perfect. We left Montana clutching several bottles of wine, due for consumption later this week, no doubt, and two Montana T-shirts and went merrily on our way. Well I certainly did, but poor David had to drive

Back on the road, we continued our journey to

My Travels with Wheely

Kaikoura. The drive was along a coastal road which was drop dead, breathtakingly beautiful. David spotted a seal nestling in the rocks so we stopped to look, it was so sweet. As your eyes became accustomed to the grey seal against the grey rocks we began to see more of them; in fact, there were hundreds of them, and ah, but they were so lovely.

The sea was made even more majestic as we watched the change in the weather conditions. It was really closing in and the sea seemed to be getting angrier. Being mindful of sea conditions, it reminded me again how much you should respect it.

We arrived in Kaikoura with no accommodation pre-booked; don't know for the life of me why I point this out because nothing in New Zealand had been pre-booked, apart from the bus and ferry crossing. No problem; we found a nice-looking campsite offering good clean accommodations. We settled in for the evening, and it was now dark and dank outside. We had absolutely no idea what the surrounding area was like.

Day Forty-nine

A new morning had arrived, and wow, it was utterly breathtaking, with the mountains on one side and the ocean on the other. I felt as if we must have died and gone to heaven overnight; the views were just stunning. The sun shined and we sat and had our coffee, watching the sun glisten on the snow-capped mountains, I felt very content and, dare I say it, happy to be alive.

Today we were going quad biking. Well why on Earth not? Whilst there wasn't a hope in hell of getting me on a quad bike, I would have to settle for something called the Argo, which was an eight–wheel, all-terrain vehicle. David was immensely excited, because he had never been on a quad bike before. In fact, he'd never really recovered from the fact that I did it some years ago and he never had, so finally now it was his chance to get even. Don't get me wrong, it's not that he's remotely competitive, but it was just something I had done and he had not, and I concluded it was just one of those male things.

We made our way, on the bus, to Glenstrae Farm travelling along the coastal road and up through the hills. Greeted by Alistair, his wife, Annette, and their son, David, they quickly introduced David to the quad bike and he skipped off like a happy thing toward it. Men can be very quirky at times. Whilst Annette ran through the operation side and safety aspects with David, all

My Travels with Wheely

of which he must master before he was allowed to go anywhere, Alistair turned his attention to mc. He was a sweet and friendly man and proceeded to say, "Bloody hell, Nicky, it's a bloody awful shame that you're in a bloody wheelchair. I'll make bloody sure that you bloody enjoy yourself in the Argo," and did he fulfil his promise. Yes, he certainly "bloody" well did.

They had approximately sixteen hundred acres of land handed down through several generations of his family which was used for farming cattle, sheep, and their relatively new venture, quad biking; what a brilliant idea. We were taken over their land and treated to the most fantastic views of the Kaikoura coastline. I thought I'd died and gone to heaven. No I hadn't, I only did that the other day. Because Alistair and I sometimes had to travel on a slightly different route from the quad bikes, Alistair was able to swing the Argo around, and he jumped out and took some action shots of David. Oh, he'd like looking at those when we got home.

We stopped at their log cabin somewhere amongst the sixteen hundred acres, and it was the most picturesque setting for a mid morning coffee. It certainly knocked Starbucks into a "cocked hat." Alistair offered us tea, and we both declined in favour of coffee, although he was somewhat taken aback as he thought all Brits only drank tea; for a moment he was lost for words.

The sun filtered through the trees and we drank our coffee, chatted, and laughed before heading off to finish our journey. This was truly a brilliant day.

Nicky Dalladay

What more could a girl want after such an exhilarating day? On the way to the farm I caught sight of a shop called Pacific Jewels, a mental note was made of this and would be stored in the brain for later use. As later had now arrived the information from my brain was retrieved, if there was one thing that I said I was going to buy on our travels, it would have to be some pieces of traditional New Zealand Paua shell jewellery. So naturally, we found ourselves in the shop, and I was delighted with my purchases.

Tonight we threw a steak on the barbie and opened a lovely bottle of wine. What more could one wish for? Ah, there was just one thing; another bottle of wine would go down as a treat.

E-mails Received

Sorry, still no luck receiving you newsletters. Anyway hope you're both well and having a fantastic time. SC

It's so great to get all your news. It all sounds *sooo* exciting. I'm so glad that you're making the most of it all. We've been enjoying those perfect early spring sunshine-filled days although cold, and the primroses and daffodils are peeping through in a riot of colour. Wonderful! I've forgotten when you're coming back home, but we're looking forward to seeing you again soon. JB

Ah, spring has sprung, and we will indeed miss all the daffs etc, but never mind, I'm sure we'll get over it.

My Travels with Wheely

The Argo versus The Quad Bike

Day Fifty

Today we bade farewell to Kaikora and made our way toward Hanmer Springs. The sun shined and it was another glorious day; this country was a very pretty place. We located a nice campsite, David unloaded the bus once more, and we sat in the afternoon sun enjoying a cup of tea and a biscuit. Yes, it has to be said that we Brits, on occasion, do enjoy a cuppa in the afternoon. It was lovely but certainly very windy, so much so that my biscuit took flight and off it went; oh well, good for the diet. We went and explored our new surroundings a little, and this was an easy day where we merely enjoyed the vistas and breathed in the beautiful fresh air. We were just happy to be.

There weren't many shops here but we did find a men's clothes shop, and I urged the ever-so-reluctant David to go and take a look. David certainly doesn't have the shopping genes that I possess, and I coaxed him to try things on. It was very cold, although sunny, and I tentatively suggested that he try on a rather nice Merino wool jumper, which was designed to lock in body heat and a reversible black and khaki body. Goodness me, he really made a meal out of shopping! It took the rest of the day, and in fact I would go as far as to say it must be like kitting out a little boy for his first day at school. However, I am delighted to report he finally parted with some money, paid for his clothes, and was evidently

My Travels with Wheely

pleased with his purchases, so it was well worth it.

He has a sort of phobia about shopping and never thinks he needs anything new because his clothes have not worn out. Get a grip. When did need ever come into anything you buy? You buy because you like something, that is all there is to it, men!

The young man in the shop was pleasant and helpful and as we so often do we got chatting. He was interested to learn about where in New Zealand we were travelling to and we mentioned that our next port of call was Greymouth. He certainly wasted no time recommending we leave this out, as according to him, it was as grey as it sounded. Ah, there is a god after all; there was reputedly one place in this country that wasn't beautiful, and I couldn't believe it. If there was one place we should visit it must be Punakaiki. He thought it was gorgeous there and promptly wrote it down for us. We said our goodbyes and exited the shop into the now evening sun.

Day Fifty-one

Now en route for our impromptu visit to Punakaiki, we hit upon Greymouth and cannot really verify the young man's opinion of this place. He so undersold it as a worthy destination that we just drove through and carried on without stopping, although on our limited sightings from the bus, he appeared to be right, it did indeed look quite grey.

We arrived just outside Punakaiki late morning and once again we couldn't appreciate our surroundings. It was another dark and dank day with the worst type of rain you could encounter, drizzle. In reality, all rain gets you wet, but this type is sort of nothing. The accommodation was quite pleasant, with motel rooms next to an inn, though not quite the sort of inn you would find at home. Nevertheless it had good beer, so David was pleased, and they actually served decent food.

During lunch the weather changed completely, and the drizzle stopped, the clouds disappeared, and the sun shined — what luck. We stepped outside and this was yet another beautiful place, so we decided to hotfoot it to Punakaiki. Our young man in the shop was right, Punakaiki was spectacular, and it was a fabulous drive again along the coastal road. I'd quite like to say that at times it got boring, but there was very little about this country's scenery that was boring, that is no word of a

My Travels with Wheely

lie.

Punakaiki is home to some amazing pancake cliffs, and they were just like a plate of layered pancakes, yum, and the thought of pancakes passes through my mind but I would have to wait until the USA for that one. The small area had been so well thought out and there was the most spectacular vegetation to wander through. In between the pancake cliffs were blowholes. Now, I'd never seen these before and was fascinated as they ejected thirty feet high bursts of water as the waves came crashing in; what a fantastic sight.

The bus made one of its many stops; we stopped and had a coffee, admiring the scenery before heading back to the motel. Into the inn for supper, during which a lady came to our table, once she had established we were visitors here, and she produced a census form for us to complete. I guessed it must be the same the world over as it was a legal requirement to do this. It actually transpired that anybody who was in New Zealand on Tuesday night 7 March, it was compulsory to fill in this form.

We looked at the document and decided that the people who lived here must be very clever; we could hardly understand it and immediately sought help to complete it. Glad to find it was not just us, the local people in the inn were just as thick; we managed to complete it and left it at the bar, as instructed, only to discover that it was a little ironic as only half the visitors actually bother to fill it in. It just demonstrated to me that bureaucracy reigned wherever you were in the world, and whilst we considered it to be a complete waste of time, at least we

Nicky Dalladay

had done our duty.

The inn was very busy, but there was something missing, laughter. So we took to the outdoors for a smoke and discovered that this was where the atmosphere of the place really was. Outside was where all the smokers were congregated, and we chatted and laughed with the natives — well, the landlord, the guy who had served coffee at the blowholes, and the local cop.

Day Fifty-two

Back on track now, on our rough guide that we had originally made, we travelled toward Franz Joseph. We arrived at our destination and it was heaving down with rain. We certainly were going through a variety of weather conditions. It was a little odd and was not dissimilar to arriving in Austria for a winter skiing holiday; apart from the fact it was raining, there were no Austrians and certainly no lederhosen. However, there were a lot of Australians, which is the one thing that is plentiful in a ski resort.

By early evening the rain had stopped and the skies were clear, so we went for a beer and enjoyed watching the sunset. We were staying on a nice campsite with an en suite bathroom; our nights spent sleeping on the bus were now a dim and distant memory.

Our new location really seemed to be a backpacker's paradise. Either that or you would be quite forgiven for thinking it was a refugee camp. Nonetheless, we were amused to see clothes strewn over the balconies, unsure whether they were trying to dry them from being washed or airing them so they didn't have to wash them. Students were quite amusing to watch as they had a lovely knack of thinking they were the first to ever do anything. Oops, I'm now sounding as though I'm a stone-age pensioner and I'm not, honest. They were young and obviously having fun, and I think a little part of me was slightly envious as I watched their carefree abandon. Oh to be a student with very few responsibilities and hardly a care in the world.

Tonight we ventured out to forage for food — well, walk to the nearest restaurant — and consumed what can only be described as a fairly average meal; they were obviously used to catering to impoverished students, when quantity counts far more than quality.

Without warning, David turned to me and said that I amazed him. Why would he say that? Perhaps it was because I genuinely was a "right royal pain in the arse"? The man I know and love looked at me tenderly with a face devoted with love for me, and just said, "I'm in total admiration of you, the way you just put up with everything and just carry on with life. I don't know anyone else who would deal with it as well as you." Blimey, he doesn't half come out with things when you least expected it, rather than quitting whilst he was ahead, he then repeated himself, saying again, "I'm amazed that you put up with everything." I couldn't resist saying, "Don't put yourself down; you're not such a difficult person to live with," and he simply replied, "I asked for that".

Not sure if I've bleated on about the standard of disabled bathrooms yet, but I'm almost certain I will have done, so please forgive me if this seems a little bit self-indulgent. Who on Earth is tasked with the important job of meeting disabled requirements, particularly in bathrooms? It sure as hell isn't someone who has ever had the pleasure of sitting in a wheelchair even for the briefest

My Travels with Wheely

of moments to check the mirrors. Picture this if you can. I've managed, with David's help, to take a shower; I have to sit on the toilet because there's no chair, and he helps me to dry and dresses me, all which is absolutely fine, between us the mission has been accomplished.

This is now the moment where it all falls apart. I transferred to Wheely to go to the sink and clean my teeth and comb my hair, only I couldn't see myself as the mirror seemed to be about two feet higher than I was sitting. Great if you can stand long enough to be able to do this, but I couldn't. In essence, what this boiled down to was that the only things I could do for myself, someone had taken away my right to do them. I was unable to look in the mirror. Once again, this led me to think that it was assumed that a disabled person does not take pride in her appearance and had absolutely no taste, and I would run the risk of looking like a twat just because I couldn't see what my hair was like.

Ah, but I have just realised there is an upside to being a female. Can you imagine a man in a wheelchair shaving? It could be like the chainsaw massacre in the bathroom every morning.

These relatively small episodes in life both angered and annoyed me. I have had to give up so much already. There was just no need for this, since the situation could be resolved and remedied very easily, if anyone had the decency to think their designs through.

E-mail Received

I still have not set the alarm off; it seems a bit like a miracle…how are you? Think it is soon time for a little update message from the DallAwayDays. Getting homesick? Fed up with the sun? I wish you a continuous great trip and looking forward to all the stories and pictures and most of all YOU. MK

Without wishing to sound unkind or ungrateful, I was absolutely amazed to hear our house alarm hadn't gone off; otherwise, there would have been panic and mayhem.

Day Fifty-three

Behold, again it was gorgeous today and we knew that we would be able to take the provisionally booked light aircraft flight over the glaciers. Knowing full well that unlike the students, we would not be able to trek over them, we had found a much better option. If the conditions were as grim as yesterday it just wouldn't have happened, which would have been a great shame as the glaciers were the real reason for visiting Franz Joseph.

Lady luck appeared to be still on our side and we made haste for the airfield for our Air Safaris tour. Damn it all, I was put in the back this time, but at least we all had a window seat. We waved goodbye to Wheely who was, once again, left on the tarmac until our return. We took to the skies and hovered, or whatever a light aircraft does, over Mount Cook and the Tasman, Fox, and Franz Josef Glaciers. The sight was awesome. Perhaps this is an overused expression but it tends to say it all, especially when one doesn't have sufficient words to describe something.

How a glacier could be quite so spectacular, I wasn't entirely sure. Perhaps it could be that it's something to do with the sheer expanse and the crisp whiteness tinged with a glacial blue. Whatever it was, it was magnificent. We flew over Mount Cook, which was so impressive you really felt you could lean out the window and touch it,

Nicky Dalladay

so luckily the windows didn't open. All in all we were in the air for about fifty minutes for this spectacular and inspirational flight, another truly memorable experience.

In a way I found this reminiscent of our visit to the glaciers in Argentina. Whilst they were not the same bright glacial blue colour, they were impressive in their sheer size. Each day seemed to get better and better. How long could this continue? There was still a load more for us to see and do, but we were so incredibly lucky to have this ahead of us.

The bus was loaded up for the umpteenth time; onward we must go and hit the road for the next destination, Haast. We arrived and were a little flummoxed as to why on Earth anyone would really want to come here. Don't get me wrong; the drive to get here was the customary beautiful one that we had now taken for granted, and Haast itself was pleasant enough. What seemed to be missing were the gorgeous lakes to sit and gawp at. I spotted a supermarket and jokingly suggested to David that perhaps it was the reason people should want to stay here, but funnily enough he didn't agree with me and certainly didn't think that was a good enough reason. I didn't expect him to agree really.

Well, we were here now, and it was far too late to change our minds and look for elsewhere, so we jolly well had to lump it and like it. As we were running low on our provisions, we decided to pop to the supermarket for tonight's supper. Well, when I said supermarket, it was not quite like your average high street supermarket that

My Travels with Wheely

we know and loathe for their existence in destroying our small towns, but that's another story. No, it was more like a very downmarket version of 7 Eleven, if that's at all possible. Perhaps more like a 3.5 Eleven would be nearer the mark. It was a very peculiar little shop, and if the few residents of Haast had to rely on this to stock their larders, I felt very sorry for them.

We had planned to buy some pâté and French bread to accompany a rather nice bottle of red wine we had back at the ranch, or rather bus. We wandered around the supermarket aimlessly, and it has to be said we were slightly put off by the cats nestling between the food. Consequently, there was so little there that you would want to put in your mouth that we found ourselves settling for some cheddar cheese and biscuits. Oh, and I found a rather nice pair of earrings at the till to buy, so at least I would feel dressed up.

Whilst on the subject of food, I haven't yet mentioned that our diet in New Zealand largely consisted of cheese and crackers. We did manage to find a few nice places to eat whilst travelling on the road, but they did seem to be few and far between. By this time, I had begun to feel like Wallace & Gromit with the amount of cheese I was consuming. Cheese was all well and good and I certainly didn't have a problem eating it, but the waist band on my trousers was starting to complain, and they were getting rather too snug for my liking.

Back at the campsite, David did what he did best, the laundry, hardly glamorous but a necessity so he trundled off leaving me to do what I do best, chat with the natives.

Nicky Dalladay

There were two bikers in the chalet next to us and they told me they were from Auckland. Apparently, they frequently took off and left their wives for two weeks while they "did their own thing." For some reason I originally thought they were gay. They really liked each other and had a huge amount of respect for one another and were clearly very good friends.

I was talking about the formation of the wonderful stars that we had seen and one of the bikers asked me if I had realized that I was looking at the Milky Way. According to them, New Zealand is one of the very few places in the world that this amazing sight can be witnessed. Somewhat pleased with myself, it turned out that I had indeed been correct in thinking this, albeit it had been a complete guess on my part.

My Travels with Wheely

Glacier Flight

Day Fifty-four

We departed Haast still wondering why we had actually gone there, other than to buy a pair of earrings of course. The bus and its load took to the road once more and made its way to Wanaka.

We had not originally planned to go there but it was at the suggestion of Alistair, you know who I mean — "Well bloody hell you have got to go to bloody Wanaka it's so bloody nice there you'll love it" — yes, that's right, the Alistair who gave us a thrilling day out on the quad bikes. Anyway, we set off and it was ghastly weather, the rain was so torrential that we could hardly see the spectacular scenery but knew it would be as beautiful as on previous drives, it was by now a given.

Getting nearer to our destination we passed by Lake Wanaka, when we saw the most fabulous sight, a complete rainbow. We had never seen one before, a complete one that is, and we tried to take a photograph but sadly it didn't come out. We would have to rely on our memories. Oh, dear.

Well we arrived, and whilst it was still precipitating rather heavily you could instantly see why Alistair had recommended that we come here. It was outstanding and captivating natural beauty. It was rather busy, which struck us as strange; we had become accustomed to not really seeing many people. We consulted our rough

My Travels with Wheely

itinerary and gathered that is was in fact the weekend, which explained the large number of people around. There was the annual A&P show on as well. With travelling so much we didn't once pay any attention to such mundane things like what day of the week it was.

There was no availability on any of the campsites, and it was looking like we would have to move on, but suddenly I saw somewhere that looked fantastic. It was a stunning alpine lodge and it appeared that the owners had been let down, and yes, they had the most incredible suite available. Being the shrewd businessman he was, Roger, the owner, quickly worked out that by letting us have the suite for the same cost as a normal room he would at least make some money. We went into the suite and it was exquisite; how nice to taste a bit of luxury again. Oh yes, we intended to enjoy every minute of our stay; there was no doubt about that.

Day Fifty-five

Guess what? The weather was stunning again and the sky was a brilliant blue with not a single cloud in sight. This had become the normal bad weather whilst travelling followed by sunshine on arrival. We were certainly being blessed by the weather gods. We walked down the hill, and poor David would have to push me back up again on the way home, best not remind him of that. We got to the edge of the lake and it was finally now that I realised I must be a cat. Why else would I be experiencing all these lives? I have died and gone to heaven once again. It is, without a shadow of a doubt, stunningly gorgeous.

As we walked by the lake we just enjoyed the moment. I reminded myself of the importance of seizing every bit of happiness when possible. There were countless occasions when life was not so wonderful that it was absolutely imperative you make the most of the good times when you could.

We stopped for lunch, and before heading back we wandered through the A&P show, that is to say an Agriculture & Produce show, which appears to be very big in New Zealand. There were lots of cows and sheep around, farm machinery, and horse events.

Whilst at the show, we bumped into a young couple we had shared the ferry crossing with, and they were travelling for six months, which made our three months

My Travels with Wheely

look like a poor effort. They were foot passengers on the boat and she was quite glad to have run into us as she had wondered what had happened to the vehicle passengers, so we filled them in.

Day Fifty–six

Wanaka was indeed an idyllic place to have visited great scenery: next to the water, wonderful accommodation, lovely restaurants, a fabulous ladies boutique (oh did I not mention that little spending spree? Clearly not), and to top it all a piece of New Zealand tradition, the A&P show. We were now heading for Queenstown but en route stopped at Brannock Burns to view vineyards, and we passed through Mount Difficulty uncertain as to why it was difficult but it was another vineyard. I now thought that there more vines than sheep here, this country really is a lamb and wine lover's delight. At dinner we actually chose a Mount Difficulty wine, a Pinot Noir, delicious.

We drove through a lovely place called Arrow Town, which looked absolutely beautiful. It did cross our minds that perhaps we should stay there but decided against it and continued our journey to Queenstown. Glad we had made the right decision. Queenstown was wonderful and we had gone from staying at relatively small places that it made a nice change to stay in a town that was fairly big. There were certainly many more people around than we had seen before and an awful lot more activity; it was terrific.

With no end of water activities available, you were certainly not going to sit idling your time away. In fact, we had not been there for more than half an hour and were

My Travels with Wheely

already booked for a tandem paragliding flight to "take us high and stay dry." Magical. We were extended about six hundred feet from the boat and felt we were on top of the world with a clear view of the panorama around us. We caught sight of Wheely on the jetty and felt like we had temporarily abandoned him. I wouldn't dream of doing that to my trusted friend, and I needed him too much. Up in the air together enjoying the sun and do you know what? It just didn't matter one single jot that I couldn't walk; the feeling of freedom was enough for me. I squealed with sheer delight. The experience was an amazing one and lasted for what seemed a long time, and when it was over the men on the boat lifted me up to the jetty like a delicate flower to reunite me with Wheely. What lovely people.

For the next two nights we had splashed out and booked into a hotel. Why? Because we decided that we could and for us the location was perfect right next to the lake. Ah, but we were booked into a disabled room and true to form it had to be without a shadow of doubt the worst room in the hotel. Where was the stunning view of the lake? Perhaps it was adjacent to the sodding car park we were looking at? All the other rooms that we could see had balconies with doors that opened to the big outside world, but oh no, not in this room, you were not allowed any fresh air. Did they seem to think there was a possibility of hurling myself out the window? This is where the two allocated disabled rooms were and this is where I must stay. Nice, eh? I chastised myself. Had I forgotten that I was no longer allowed to have any feelings or taste since entering the life of a wheelchair user? Silly old me.

We had just been for the most spectacular dinner sat

overlooking the lake — fabulous food and exemplary service — what could be better? Not a lot, really. It was a perfect evening and we casually strolled back toward the hotel when something took our eye: a chocolate shop. There was a man in the window and he was spreading his chocolate lovingly onto a slab, waiting for it to dry. Once dry he then curled it up to resemble a flake, and as we entered the shop he handed me one of the flakes that he had to reject because it wasn't perfect enough to sell. Yum, sod the "minute on the lips a lifetime on the hips" business; this was melt-in-the-mouth gorgeous. As if by magic, we were transformed into kids in a candy shop. It all looked so appealing, so we looked at the delights on offer. Looking obviously transpired into selecting, and naturally we bought it. Well, it was hard not to, really. We told ourselves it would complement our coffee back at the hotel. Yeah, who were we kidding?

We passed a Louis Vuitton shop and I hazarded a guess that we would be visiting it tomorrow just to see how much the prices were for market research purposes. David laughed but I couldn't think why. We reflected on what a lovely day this had been, sipped our coffee, and indulged ourselves with the delicious chocolate. Never mind, I could always burn it off tomorrow.

E-mail Received

Nice getting your news about your travels. AMN

Short but sweet and straight to the point; that's my girl.

Day Fifty-seven

We had now been on the road for eight weeks but it felt as though it had been much longer, which was a good thing. We had already seen so much I felt enlightened and educated; it was a great feeling, particularly from one who didn't receive the benefit of a good education. I did go to a convent in my earlier years, but you know what they say about convent girls! Anyway, I seem to be digressing. To date, there was absolutely nothing materialistic that I missed at home, which surprised me a little, but there you go.

You know I mentioned that I would be able to burn the calories off from the previous evening. I didn't actually mean me. Believe it or not, nothing would give me greater pleasure than to stretch my calves by walking up a steep hill. No, it was David who today demonstrated he could push me up a very steep hill and burn many calories. Is there no justice in the world? He's so slim. Anyway, the purpose of this mammoth journey up the hill was to go on the Skyline gondola, restaurant, and luge to enjoy some spectacular panoramic views of Queenstown, or maybe not.

The Skyline had promised us some spectacular views and was reputed to be the steepest lift in the Southern hemisphere. It allegedly boasted the best views in the region from their special observation decks.

Nicky Dalladay

It took a fair amount of wrestling to get me into the cable car, my legs had "gone off on one" and were like rods of iron that just would not bend. I sometimes thought it would be easier to snap them in half so you could just throw them in. Meanwhile, Wheely was the recipient of some first-class treatment and was placed with great care neatly in his own cable car. Blimey, must make a note, perhaps I should come back in my next life as a wheelchair. You certainly seem to get looked after better, at least until you go into the hold of an aeroplane.

We reached the top, only to find we were prevented from walking around the platform because there was no wheelchair access and only steps, and I don't do steps. To say we were a little annoyed would be a bit of an understatement. All I could think of was that it was akin to having a room with a side ocean view, where you were only afforded the merest glimpse of the sea and that you have been denied the opportunity of seeing the whole picture. Feeling we were justified in making a complaint we did just that and approached a lady who we felt sure must be some sort of official, simply because she was wearing a badge, so she had to be.

Clearly she was left out of the personality section when being put together, as well as the humour one and possibly the humane one…where on Earth did they dredge her up from? "Mrs. Humourless" was positively aghast when we informed her that we should have been told when buying our tickets that I wouldn't be able to see much. Mrs. Humourless was doubly aghast when I proffered the suggestion that I should only been charged at a concession rate for half the view. She couldn't see

My Travels with Wheely

why anyone would be worthy of a concession, if someone can't walk just shoot 'em. Not that she actually said that of course, but I had interpreted what I imagined she was thinking. We seemed to be going from bad to worse, and she was having none of this and she made no attempt to offer any form of apology no matter how insincerely she could have done it. She merely looked away, which was an even bigger insult. Now David is by no means a violent man but I had to restrain him, because he was very angry. I suppose if we had consulted the skyline map, warning bells should have struck us that there were no disabled toilets. My advice is, if you have any form of a walking difficulty, do not bother with this activity; it deserves a very wide berth.

We put this behind us and moved swiftly on and the challenge was laid down to search for some real fun, and boy did we find it. Back toward the bay where we did paragliding yesterday we saw an advertisement for the Kawarau Jet Boat on Lake Wakatipu. Going through the tranquil beauty of the willow-lined Kawarau River, the jet boat then speeds into the shallow, fast-moving narrow braids of the Shotover River, highlighting the diversity of Queenstown's waterways. This looked as though it would do very nicely, thank you, and we felt sure this would hit the spot.

Fourteen of us were kitted out with life jackets, and again I was gently carried down the steps in Wheely to the boat and tipped in, no, I mean helped in. We had to hold onto a bar for safety and were already snuggled up to our neighbours, so there was no danger of a body going overboard. Phew, that was a relief, and off we went.

Nicky Dalladay

The speed was incredible and again, I squealed with sheer delight as I did when we all got drenched. The adrenaline kicked in and reminded me of the long gone days of skiing down a black run; this was so exhilarating and a fantastic experience. Back on land I sat and dripped dry over Wheely. Well, he can't always have his cake and eat it.

A quick turnaround at the hotel and we made our way to the restaurant we had booked for dinner, aptly named the Bathhouse Cafe and Fine Food Restaurant. The location was perfectly positioned right on the beach of the lake, and the restaurant was designed to look like a crown. It was quite small inside but ever so beautiful. The interior was impeccable and each table was laid out with lots of cutlery and glasses — I hoped I knew what they were all for — and adorned with the finest table linen I had ever seen. Suddenly, we both felt that we were in the wrong place and it was way too grand for us humble travellers, but fortunately, we managed to get over that one quite quickly when we were shown to our seats.

The service was top notch and we could not find fault with anything. Not that we were looking for anything to find fault with. We spent a considerable amount of time looking at the wine list as there was now plenty on it that we recognised and had actually been lucky enough to have already tasted. We proceeded to order a wine from the Waikoura area, which borders Queenstown. Shortly, the sommelier returned without a bottle, and us that was the only wine left off their delivery earlier today, what bad luck. Back to the drawing board and we go for a wine from the Gibbston Valley a Pinot Noir, as we had driven

My Travels with Wheely

through the region a few days previously. Incidentally, we had developed a liking for Pinot Noir the more we tasted, and believe me, we had tasted an awful lot. The evening turned out to be a very special one and we both enjoyed it immensely. In fact, it was probably safe to say it was the best meal out we had had since our travels began.

Day Fifty-eight

The bus was loaded again and the two carefree hippies, the Moonshines, were on their way. Although we weren't entirely sure where we were going, it would be in the vague direction of Christchurch. How very strange. We seemed to be backtracking at the moment, which could mean one of two things: David had a cunning plan, or this could be a very long day; I felt it could be the latter. We broke our journey for a cuppa, cheese, and biscuits at Lake Pukataiki; no lay-by for us, oh no, our view was Mount Cook in all its glory, snow capped with a beautiful blue lake in front of it. We looked at each other and said, "We've been there."

We stayed for much longer than we anticipated, largely due to the fact that I had managed to attract a truck driver to chat with, which was quite clever of me really as I hadn't even set foot off the bus. I very much enjoyed talking to him, and he told me he had driven all the way from Auckland to do some filming for a commercial. He informed me that this was his first visit to the South Island, and he was quite excited and totally in awe of the beauty of this part of his country he had never seen before. I felt compelled to ask him if he would like me to take a picture of him standing in front of Mount Cook, and he smiled sweetly at me and said thank you that would be nice.

My Travels with Wheely

Arriving at Lake Tekapo, we instantly decided this was where we must stop but only if we could find somewhere to stay, which had a stunning view of the lake, and as luck would have it we found such a place. Lake Tekapo is described as a delightful alpine village in the heart of the South Island. Apparently, it is a skiing resort in winter and an aquatic playground in the summer. The landscape is outstanding and is often described as a jewel, the water is a magnificent intense turquoise, and we had never seen such beautiful colour water before.

David decided it was time to do another washing load and off he went, only moments later he returned a little disgruntled as he had been unable to perform his task. The washing machine was broken. Oh dear, I shall have to tell him my one and only joke to make him laugh. It was early evening and we sat outside our cabin had a glass of wine and just sighed at the beauty in front of us.

Day Fifty-nine

We rose early — remember; early for us is not other people's interpretation of early — and made our way to the shower. Today was the first time in many a year that a shower was definitely not going to happen for me. The little faded Suffolk pink plastic shower cubicle with its slippery sides had absolutely nothing for me to hold on to, that was assuming I was actually going to be able to get in it in the first place. Although we made a valiant effort to get my legs over the massive lip to get me in the shower, it began to look increasingly unlikely that we would accomplish our challenge. My legs had gone off on one again, and they were completely stiff and weren't going anywhere. Zapped of all strength we had to admit defeat, the drain had reared its ugly head again, and defeat is not something that comes easily to me. I was sure I could manage one day without a shower, it was going to be hard, though better make sure I used double the amount of deodorant. So with David clean and fresh, and smelly old me, we headed for the roads and left the picturesque Lake Tekapo behind us.

The day was really taken up by driving, and believe me, in New Zealand it was pleasurable, and although we were getting slightly more used to our beautiful surroundings, we still found ourselves expressing an ah or oh every few minutes. We stopped for a coffee and lunch on the edge of what looked like a forest, though it was a bit hard to tell here as all the vegetation was enormous.

My Travels with Wheely

I haven't mentioned this before but I had developed a new pastime, and it's called, "Let's see how many drinks you can throw over yourself in one day." Not only was it a bit frustrating, but I was worried that I might become dehydrated, as I am sure I read somewhere that you needed to swallow liquid as opposed to letting it seep through your clothes to your skin to be of any benefit. Anyway, there we were sitting and just enjoying the day, and woops, the next thing I knew I was wearing my coffee. Oh well, it might help me not to smell so much.

We arrived on the outskirts of Christchurch and stopped at a campsite in a place called Silverton, and David did his usual routine of checking out the rooms on offer. I remained on the bus and watched him go into the first room to investigate it; shortly he emerged wearing a sort of grimace on his face and a slightly upturned nose. *Interesting,* I thought. I watched him go into the second room and once more he emerged wearing pretty much the same expression, not looking good, I reckoned. "Well, Nick, there's not much in it, they're both tragic"; crikey, I knew he was a pessimist, but surely they weren't that bad. He informed me that one of them was just ever so slightly more disabled friendly than the other, so we decided to take that one. David pushed me into the room and ran away laughing. I gazed around the room and firmly believed I had stepped back in time to how I imagined a holiday camp would be back in the 1960s.

Yes it was truly hideous inside, but hey, we were only here for one night. Oh damn, I had just remembered we had booked in for two nights; oh, how the mighty had fallen.

Nicky Dalladay

We stepped inside the room a little further, and David had returned and had fortunately recovered from his mass hysteria. Right now, we appeared to be in a kitchen come dining room come sitting room, a room clearly serving many functions. Running along the back wall was a curtain. Did we think there could be nice room concealed behind it? I thought not. David giggled and drew back one curtain whilst making a fanfare noise. There was a bed and that was it. Well, to be honest, what more did you need, other than a small amount of room to be able to move around the room in? Silly me, what was I thinking? Hardly important when one was agile enough and could leap across the bed so one was able to get into it, although the one referred to obviously didn't include me.

There was also a partition wall, which was presumably not ever intended to be solid, by the look of it. It was made of hardboard and fell somewhat short of the top by a foot or so. This "palatial" bedroom was adjacent to the second bedroom, which was nowhere near as grand as the first room. The rooms indicated to me that there was a strict no-privacy policy to be adhered to.

Now our attention turned to the bathroom, and oh boy, this was hideous beyond belief, but I mustn't complain. At least they had a walk-in shower, although as you can see that was not quite enough to prevent me from going on about it.

Then there was the toilet. Shall we say this could be described as interesting? Why on Earth was there a sawn-off banister rail by the side of the toilet? Ah yes.

My Travels with Wheely

I remembered now…this was a disabled room. Why bother with the effort and expense of buying a proper securely fitted steel handrail when you could just make do with the old remnants?

Okay, the point had come that I now needed to go to the toilet, so somewhat reluctantly I rested my hand on the rail. Naturally it wobbled and nearly fell off, but that's not the best bit. Because I can't stand for long I invariably crashed down onto the pan, and this time was no different. The toilet moved and I unintentionally managed to relocate it by an inch or so. Picture this if you can: I am still sat down and David has rushed in because of the noise and gets down to the base of the toilet and grovels between my legs to see that there are no screws holding it in place. This bathroom was a death trap, make no mistake. Suffice it to say, I would remain in fear for my life every time I crashed down on this thing for the duration of our stay here.

Moving swiftly on, it was a suitable time to go hunting for the procurement of suitable fodder for supper. Oh dear, it wasn't just me, but everywhere we stopped to look at to eat resulted in developing an affliction of our noses curling up; in fact, it was less promising the further afield we ventured. We drove to New Brighton, not as nice as it sounds by any means, where we decided the only real choice available to us was fish and chips; sometimes we really know how to live.

We went to the sea where we sat in our bus like a couple of old codgers, ate, and just watched the surfers waiting for their waves; what a boring pastime. It was

Nicky Dalladay

quite late for them to be going out, but hey, they were pretty gung ho about it.

Our food attracted the gulls, and before we knew it they were swarming all over our bus and doing what they do best, how ghastly. They were incredibly tame and would come to the window to collect their chips but not so nice when all their friends descended upon us at once. *Time to go,* we thought and returned to base. Ah, the prospect of home sweet home filled us with dread.

Day Sixty

Having lefts the gulls of the previous night behind, we emerged from our accommodation only to find an invasion of ducks everywhere. It was funny watching them snuffling around for food, and the minute you dropped any crumbs they were all there, and when clearly the food had run out they would take flight. All I could think of was duck in orange sauce.

After breakfast, which was actually lunchtime by now, we clambered on the bus and headed for Christchurch. We were curious to see what sights there were on this dull and very gloomy day. Christchurch was very pleasant, although it was very strange being among so many people again. We wandered around and found the library and decided to see if we could find any newspaper coverage for 3 March, remember it was the day of our memorable ferry crossing. Expecting to see a little notice buried somewhere in the paper, imagine our surprise to discover it was headline news. We read it with great interest and realized just how lucky we had been.

We read in the papers that two thousand Cook Strait ferry passengers had their plans disrupted as gale force winds and swells of up to twelve metres forced the cancellation of the Interislander ferry service. Vehicles were adrift on the lower decks, and passengers were battered and bruised. The paper reported that the waves

223

Nicky Dalladay

were taller than a house, seats on board were strewn all over the place, and the ferry eventually limped its way back into Picton.

We finished in the library and looked for somewhere for a late lunch, which isn't easy when you've got two fussy sods like us. Don't get me wrong; we are certainly not fussy eaters and do in fact eat the majority of things, but we would like something without chips. One of the virtues of patience is that you will eventually strike lucky, and we did: venison for David and lamb for me.

Once more we clambered back on the bus so that we could return to Butlins, oh, what deep joy. We turned the television on and watched some of the Commonwealth Games, opened a bottle of wine (our final one from Marlborough), when David's thoughts turned to preparing supper. Tonight would be no different, and we had what had become our staple diet whilst in New Zealand, toast and cheese. Although I was reliably informed that we didn't have any bread, this evening we would have our alternative menu of crackers; that'll be a nice change. That reminded me that since we had been travelling around New Zealand David hadn't once used the cooking facilities. Anyone else would think he was slacking, but I was deeply worried. I just hoped he hadn't forgotten how to cook

E-mail Received

Hope you're in good form. Just wanted to say a big "thank you" for the mini telescope and bottle of wine, very much appreciated. Rather sadly, and indicative of

My Travels with Wheely

my passing years, I have become quite interested in birds (feathered variety, of course). We get quite a few interesting specimens in the garden (alongside the occasional deer), and I now have a small reference book by the kitchen window to help me spot the lesser spotteds, etc. All this is deeply worrying, really. So, the telescope will now be located next to the breakfast bar for easy access. Looking forward to your next update. RA

How nice, a polite friend, although I was extremely concerned about the new hobby which I had obviously played a part in.

Day Sixty-one

This was our penultimate day in New Zealand, and I took a picture of David standing by the bus, as it would now be returned. On the back of the bus were the words "Maui, The Spirit of Independence," and these words would live on in my mind for an eternity. The motor home was a brilliant idea and it gave us the complete freedom we sought to go where and when we wanted to. The fact that we only slept in it for a total of four nights was neither here nor there; we had actually managed to fulfil our dream of travelling around this stunning country in the way we felt it should be done; we did it, and we are immensely proud of that. We remained carefree for the duration of our stay here and just dealt with tricky situations as and when they arose, even though the bus was not remotely disabled friendly. Who cared? We had a ball.

So to our final resting place for our stay in New Zealand, we drove into Christchurch and went and returned the bus, hung up our hippie clothes and packed our guitar, and took a taxi to the hotel. We once again found ourselves surrounded by the luxurious trappings of a hotel; lovely.

We went for a walk around the town and stopped at the market to take a look at the beautiful jewellery. Suddenly, the man selling asked where we were from,

My Travels with Wheely

and when we said the United Kingdom he rather cleverly deduced that we were indeed an awful long way from home. He was interested to learn how we had managed to travel halfway around the world in a wheelchair, a question I had asked myself many times. He said that he also used a wheelchair, although not permanently, as according to him, his legs were a bit "crook." He was rather keen to travel but understandably nervous about it, so he wanted to know all the ins and outs, and we told him. He was very encouraged by our travel service suggestions and told us that when he got home he would discuss the issue with his wife.

Funnily enough, we bumped into him the following morning. He thanked us profusely for our advice, said he was encouraged by having met us, and said they had started to plan their journey seriously and would go ahead with it. We were just pleased to be able to help.

We managed to have one final little shop at Naturally McDonald New Zealand, somewhere that stocked Possum/Merino sweaters in abundance that were actually made here and not in China. Whilst in Australia, possums were a protected species. It is the opposite in New Zealand where they are considered an absolute pest; hence all the possum wear for sale. Anyway, that's by the by, and I decided I was going to purchase a possum cardigan trimmed with pure New Zealand lambskin leather. David at first was muttering on about how expensive it was, so I tactically ignored him and carried on looking; always the best way, I find. In view of the fact that he was being totally ignored by my good self, I saw him skulking off into the men's department.

Nicky Dalladay

I had chosen my cardigan and went to see what he was up to. Would you believe he was now trying on possum sweaters? Sadly, they were all just too large, and he resembled a child trying on his brother's hand-me-downs that despite any growing he should do would never fit him properly. It was rapidly becoming clear there was not going to be a little shopping experience for him today. His lip pouted and there was the first sign of a sulk that I had never seen from him before, which in my view was deeply unattractive.

We dined at the hotel tonight and savoured every mouthful of the delicious New Zealand lamb we had both ordered, accompanied by a rather splendid bottle of wine.

Sixth E-mail
Bumper Edition

Well, where to start? The DallAwayDays have landed in New Zealand — to be more specific, Auckland. It's quite late in the evening and we take an airport shuttle bus to the hotel, big mistake as the driver starts acting like some tour guide whilst we are knackered, hungry, and just need to get there. Anyway, we do eventually get there and the hotel is fabulous. It is about 22.00 and we were reliably informed that Bill Clinton was staying there, yet he didn't think to seek us out. So we hotfoot it to the bar, have a few drinks and something to eat, and eventually roll into bed at midnight plus.

Bright and early the next morning we head off back to near the airport to pick up the campervan for our adventures in New Zealand for the next twenty or so days, and boy what

My Travels with Wheely

an adventure.

From this point on and for the duration of New Zealand only, we shall be known as Mr. & Mrs. Moonshine. Why? I shall try to explain, but you need to imagine. We pick up the van and immediately feel transformed. It is as though we should be wearing caftans, Jesus sandals, have long, flowing hair, be strumming an acoustic guitar, and uttering the words groovy, man. Naturally on the van there should be a good supply of "whacky backy" purely for our consumption (or is there? Anyway, I'm afraid that you will never get to know). Right, so now you have the picture of what we are, or rather how we feel; we are in the correct attire for those long-gone hippie days. We head off in our Volkswagen dormobile, now renamed the "bus," in a cloud of eternal love for anything that breathes — or doesn't, as the case may be.

We set our co-ordinates for Waihi Beach, which is situated on a spectacular peninsula with a harbour on one side and sea on the other. The sun was shining, and we spent our first night being at one with nature; that is to say nearly, since it was just too cold to bear all. We look up and just gaze at the stars whilst lying on our not-so-comfortable bed. On our first night we already find ourselves asking how on Earth we are we going to sleep on this for another twenty nights.

The following morning, at the crack of dawn — well, ten-ish — we head for Rotorua to spend the next two nights staying beside the Blue Lake. We have been blessed; the weather remains good, and still at one with nature we spent the next two nights sleeping on the bus and gazing

Nicky Dalladay

at the stars, or more specifically, the Milky Way! I think it is, I have never actually seen it before, but David in his infinite wisdom emphatically says it is not.

We made our way through Taupo, stopping for lunch by the lake, and then we decided to take a left turn and ended up at the Huka Falls. What a true delight that was. The water was a magnificent glacial blue.

We were making our way to Napier for a two-night stay. We decided that we were fed up with freezing our various bits off on the bus and opted for the comfort (all things being relative) of a cabin on the campsite, so we could be half of one with nature. At Napier, we went on a wine tour of six vineyards, ending at the Mission. Sounds like the temperance society, but believe me it was far from it, hic.

We set off with plans to go to Martinborough but never made it. Well we did but had to pass through as there was no accommodation available, so we just kept on driving with gay abandon in our "luv truck" until we got to Wellington. We kept on driving to Lower Hutt, Upper Hutt, but there was nada. "No hutts available" for us. Fortunately, we eventually got lucky (lucky probably the wrong description), but we found a motel to rest our weary heads.

North Island was indeed beautiful whichever way you turned and very much deserves a second visit with a lot more time being spent there.

Because we arrived earlier than expected in Wellington we decided to change our scheduled ferry crossing from

My Travels with Wheely

4 March to 3. Oops, big mistake. Looking at it another way, the sudden change of plan had its good points and its bad points.

The ferry crossing to South Island is one that we will remember for the rest of our days. It was a sunny morning, quite windy, but nice. We were loaded on first just after the heavy trucks, the reason being so that we could access the lift to the upper decks with ease. The voyage commenced and all seemed well, even though we thought the quantities of "sick bags" being put out was rather on the high side. But we thought, *I suppose people can feel a little sick on a boat.* We ventured outside to take in the air and view the spectacular scenery. All was beautiful, the waves were rolling quite high, the wind blowing strong, the sea spray fairly wet, but we thought little of it. More importantly, what on Earth was going on with my hair? It was truly a bad day for maintaining the coiffure look.

Suddenly we noticed that people started to change colour and were having trouble standing as the boat was rolling and the swell getting greater. One by one people began to disappear inside, leaving only about five of us outside. It soon transpired that we were the only passengers who didn't get seasick. Then with an almighty lunge, the boat rolled. It rolled further and further and further, and in fact far more than the captain or for that matter we had expected. Without warning, Wheely and I lunged into the side railings, and the remaining four passengers followed suit, clinging onto Wheely for dear life. At this point it felt like we were at forty-five degrees to the sea, and it appeared to be so close that you could have touched it.

Nicky Dalladay

Phew, what an absolute bender of a trip. I assume it would be a better high than any drug could possibly give you. The journey is supposed to take round about three hours, or so but in these conditions and with us facing a twelve metre swell; we were not going to go anywhere very quickly. The captain informed us that we would be deviating from our route and would be taking a different route to look for calmer waters, and that the voyage would now take some nine hours. *Marvellous,* we thought. At one point we were told that we all (the five of us that is) had to come inside, sit on the floor, brace ourselves, and keep our fingers crossed for an attempted 270 degree turn., For heaven's sake, we're British, aren't we!

We arrived in Picton where the ferry docked, but only the foot passengers were allowed off. It then transpired that there was a serious amount of damage to the vehicles below. We eventually got down there at 23.45 to see total carnage. All of the campervans had been trashed, apart from one. Would you believe the one untouched campervan was ours? Purely because we had parked behind the trucks and not alongside them like the other campervans had done, it escaped harm.

As you will imagine this was a breathtaking journey in more ways than one, but finally it was over. We now wend our way to the campsite some two minutes down the road. No luxury for us, though we find ourselves spending our fourth and thank god final night on the bus. We awoke the next morning to find ourselves the talk of the campsite. It wasn't until later that day that the full realization of just what had actually happened on the ferry sunk in, and we both felt quite sick.

My Travels with Wheely

Anyway, the voyage now behind us, we pick up the guitar, continue strumming, throw our long locks of hair back, and go along our travelling way.

We drive through Marlborough and make a stop (it would be rude not to) at the House of Montana for a spot of lunch and a wee wine-tasting session; jolly lovely it was too. In fact, it was so lovely that we felt obliged to purchase several bottles for the journey.

We continued on a beautiful coastal drive to Kaikoura, home for the next two nights. We went quad biking — well, David did — and I was in the bouncing bomb, a contraption called the Argo. We had terrific fun and saw some of the most spectacular scenery we have ever seen in our life; oh my this is a truly very beautiful country. From here we journey through torrential rain to Hanmer Springs and then on to Punakaiki to see the pancake rocks and blowholes. How on Earth can anywhere be this beautiful? From here we travel to Franz Josef, which really reminded me of those long-gone skiing days, sigh. Franz Joseph is home to gorgeous glaciers, and we felt somewhat obliged to take a light aircraft trip so that we could gasp and make more suitable appreciative noises.

We move onto Haast, although we're not quite sure why it seems that it has a supermarket and that's about it, and even that's c***. Can't win 'em all I suppose.

Ah and then we arrive in Wanaka, which is truly beautiful, gorgeous, wonderful, etc. and spent a glorious two nights there. Then it was on to Queenstown for another two lovely nights, a spot of paragliding, and then jet boating.

Nicky Dalladay

Oooooh, we're having such fun. Then to Lake Tekapo; oh, god more beauty, how much more can we take? We've yet to see anything horrible.

Finally, Christchurch and we pack away our hippie clothes for the time being, and David gets his hair cut for the second time on our travels. We meanwhile reflect on this beautiful country and vow to return and do it justice by spending more time here.

For those of you interested in statistics here are a few for you to ponder over. Population four million, visitors two million p.a., cows twenty million, and sheep somewhere in the region of one hundred million (I should know, I counted them, honest).

Love to everyone
The DallAwayDays
xxxx

Just before we finally depart I take time out to reflect on this spectacular visit. For us, New Zealand had been a perfect place to be. It was an exquisite country and offered a natural, unspoilt beauty. Beyond all expectations, it had a consistent charm and attractiveness that rarely faltered, and on the very odd occasion when it did, you immediately forgave it; it was but a minute blip. It was like stepping back in time, which is certainly no bad thing and yet it has managed to retain a uniqueness that most of the world has long forgotten. The people were kind, gentle, and very helpful.

The accommodation available, whilst occasionally

My Travels with Wheely

suspect, was hardly enough to alter your view of the journey back in time through New Zealand. It was indeed very quirky but hardly a showstopper.

New Zealand was truly amazing, so tranquil and calm, and I loved the feeling of being totally at peace with myself; surely I had earned that. I felt I had encountered a small change in my personality, and I almost quite liked myself. For that I was very grateful.

Life was almost certainly still going to present its hurdles, but I felt I would be able to cope a little better thanks to this invaluable and magical experience. Thank you, New Zealand, it was so worth travelling halfway around the world.

Day Sixty-two
Flight Twelve

It was time to pack up again and shove as much as we possibly could into the swollen suitcase. David performs yet another amazing accomplishment in this department, and we are ready to leave.

This short flight from Christchurch to Auckland was necessary to take us on the next step of our journey.

Flight Thirteen
Auckland to Oahu, Hawaii

We transferred our flight to continue our journey, once again full of excitement. What would our next destination hold for us?

We had now crossed the international dateline and had landed the day before we took off. I remained convinced this would confuse us for some time to come. Could this be construed as a groundhog day? Were we a day younger than the day before or were we in fact older than the day before? I was right, obviously we were very confused. So having benefited from gaining an extra day, we thought we would no doubt use it wisely. Although secretly I had my suspicions about this, I felt certain it would really go unnoticed, especially when you considered the huge amount of wasted time spent in airports and the like.

My Travels with Wheely

We had now landed in Oahu, Hawaii; welcome to America. I had cunningly forgotten it was actually part of the great USA, shame on me. We were brought back down to Earth with a sharp jolt and witnessed firsthand the inefficiencies of what America had to offer.

By now, after all, we were well-seasoned travellers, we had become well accustomed to the fact that generally I was loaded first on aeroplanes and taken off last in economy. I knew very well my place in line in the pecking order of life, and the immortal words "mustn't grumble" sprang to mind. To be honest, it was no big deal really, you just get to sit for a little longer, and I nearly forgot that sitting is something I do very well. So we were now in Hawaii and expecting our first Lei, in a manner of speaking. Well, they always received them on *Hawaii Five O,* so why should now be any different? Apparently they didn't seem to do this anymore; this must have been one of life's cost-cutting measures. Oh for goodness sake, another myth shattered before my eyes.

Our transfer coach was ready and waiting to take us to our hotel in downtown Honolulu. Now at our hotel, we discovered that it was very interesting in more ways than one. The reception area was partially covered and right next to the swimming pool. There was also a bar area, completely open to the elements, that you would expect in a sunny and warm climate, and it was the only bar in the hotel. Just to the right of the pool under cover there was a bank of Internet terminals that required dollar bills to be fed into their hungry slots. I imagined they would be very greedy things. One got the impression that Hawaii was a rather idyllic place with very little rainfall

Nicky Dalladay

and nothing but blue skies; therefore, I was inclined to think this was just perfect.

Shriek, we had just arrived in our room, which was truly hideous and resembled, I imagined, décor of the 1960s or thereabouts. Suffice it to say, it was not very good. The thought occurred to me that it was just as well we hadn't been employed by the best hotel guide. These were just my own observations and realized other people might quite like it. Curiously there were three double beds in the bedroom. so I had a wild guess that it was one for each of us and one for the luggage.

My attention was drawn back to the bedroom itself. The walls were covered with brown and orange swirls and the carpet was a sludgy green, not that any of this really mattered very much. It was not our intention to hibernate in our room, and this was sufficient reason for us not to. However, there was an upside to this gloomy room, and that was the disabled bathroom. It was not too bad, and this alone was by no means a good enough reason to keep us inside, so we took a hike to see what went on in the outside world.

E-mails Received

It sounds like New Zealand was fantastic, with no shortage of excitement! I was glad to see that we Brits continued to show the stiff upper lip in the face of adversity, made us all the more determined to get to NZ and spend a long time there. Can't believe you have been away so long and well over halfway. There is nothing much to report here apart from TB selling peerages for big loans. Is there any

My Travels with Wheely

wonder we are all becoming cynical about the morals of politics, or should I say politicians? Weather is bloody cold here and has been for more than a month, still no rain and we have a hose pipe ban from 1 April, quite incredible. Looking forward to seeing you both again when you get back home. J&JB

Great to hear the latest from the DallAwayDays, sounds like you're having a fantastic time. Our news is baby B has entered the world. All doing well, and the boys are being really helpful. S&EW

I decided that having e-mails sent back to us was very good, and, in fact, better than any newspaper. Information contained a brief update on politics, personal news, and of course the latest weather.

Day Sixty-three

Following a somewhat haphazard breakfast experience of a takeaway meal at our hotel, the food on offer fairly indescribable, we headed for the nearest Starbucks to fill up on cappuccino and double chocolate chip muffins. We really were increasing their profit margin.

With breakfast behind us, we headed straight for Waikiki Beach and enjoyed the warmth of the sun on this superb day. We strolled along the promenade, and I stopped to chat with a Polynesian woman who was wearing the most fabulous hat decorated with fruit and flowers. Whilst I made this unscheduled stop to chat, David couldn't help but wonder where this conversation was going.

I was intrigued, or just plain nosy, because she was surrounded by several pairs of shoes at her feet. They couldn't possibly be all of hers, mainly because they looked far too small. All was soon to be revealed. She told me she was a grandmother twelve times over, and whilst the children were all having a lot of fun playing in the sea she took great delight in watching them and of course guarded their shoes. This woman exuded warmth and happiness and had a most beautiful and welcoming smile; she was a delight to chat with, and I felt lucky to have met her.

We continued along our way, stopping to admire the

My Travels with Wheely

landmark of Diamond Head, which was beautiful, but sadly our view was slightly obscured by all the houses. I couldn't help but think that was indeed evidence of modern life: if there was any space available, just build on it.

News item, we had just seen our first ever happy jogger, which reminded me of something Max the tour guide/paramedic from Sydney had said: he had never taken up jogging as it looked like a miserable pastime, as they all looked thoroughly unhappy. Well, Max, I've got news for you, happy joggers did exist, even if they were in the minority.

E-mails Received

Sounds horribly scary, the boat trip, I would have been a jabbering wreck and thoroughly ill. I felt seasick on the Isle of Wight ferry once. Thanks for your fabulous updates, Nick. You've missed your vocation in life I feel. S&AM

Three weeks ago today it was a little hairy but then suddenly B was born and all is well…B is having her first outing tomorrow and after her first "reception" I've been elected to do Sunday lunch for all of us, joy. The Christening will be on 11 June, so put the date in your diary. It sounds as if you had a bit of a scare on the boat but glad to hear you had such a good time in NZ. Bet you're spending a fortune on photographs or digital whatever. Everything here is fine. I am quite busy with the local elections: believe it or not, I have "agreed" to fly the flag in a local Ward. Anyway, look forward to your next message and take care. VM

Your NZ voyage had me in stitches, and the imagery was

just great. Life is pretty routine just now, work, home, work must book a short break soon. Carry on having fun, looking forward to hearing more of your adventures. DJ

I knew that you would like NZ. It has so much to offer and is so compact. Everything is so close. You get from sunny beaches to glaciers quite quickly. In the meantime here in England I have passed my IMC. Thank god. After I had written the exam I didn't know if I would pass or fail. It is not so easy to write an exam in a second language but I survived. All the best for the rest of your world trip. PW

Every time we hear from you, your adventures get more and more exciting, though glad not to be sharing that campervan with you and the seasickness. I've heard that New Zealand is beautiful and you certainly describe it as such. You won't want to come home but at least coming to a good time of year. We're all missing you and think of you often out there somewhere. Last night was C's charity dinner and I had to sit next to MH. C introduced him with that story of me mistaking him for his cousin. Brought the house down and I nearly wore a paper bag over my head all evening. Keep those zazzy newsletters coming. NB

It was a jolly good job that friends weren't on our crossing as they would have needed more sick bags! How cool, it was excellent to have an invitation for the summer when you're on the other side of the world.

Day Sixty-four

You may remember that I mentioned Hawaii looked as though it didn't receive much rainfall, and generally they don't. That was until today. The heavens opened and it was coming down in stair rods, and neither of us had seen anything like this before. We couldn't possibly let a little bit of inclement weather put us off from venturing outside this dull and oppressive room, so we headed for our takeaway breakfast.

Bear in mind that nowhere by the pool was really sheltered, and this made for a very soggy breakfast indeed for those who fancied it. There was water everywhere, so much so that it was forming another swimming pool on its own. We peered out from behind our shelter we had managed to squeeze into to see a staff member valiantly attempting to move the water. Where it was going to go I didn't know. I actually hazarded a guess that she had received her instructions from management and had obviously been given the task of clearing this deluge. Oh well, it would certainly keep her gainfully employed for some hours to come.

Deciding that we couldn't just sit there waiting for the rain to stop we made haste to the local equivalent of a news agent. What a lucky break for us to discover they were doing a roaring trade in pack-a-macs which were selling like hotcakes before our very eyes. All was not lost

Nicky Dalladay

though, as supplies seemed to be plentiful, so we were not going to miss out on the latest fashion accessory, to our great relief.

Once we had worked out how to open the packets it should have been plain sailing from there, but no, a degree was required for assembly instructions. What did we expect for $1.00? Excellent, we were not quite as stupid as we originally thought and managed to work out what we were supposed to do with the contents and promptly put them on. I now imagined that we must look like a couple of condoms walking down the street, and rather felt that to call us "Mr. & Mrs. Condom" seemed somehow appropriate. We looked absolutely ridiculous, but at least we were relatively dry. Also, I took comfort from the fact that it was highly unlikely we would bump into anyone we knew who would see us wearing our condoms. Should that situation happen it would not be mentioned because everybody looked utterly ridiculous. Having said all that, I shall of course take it home, because you never know, they may just catch on or be of some use.

So now we were kitted out with our condoms and were set to go, we could now visit some of the shops, which of course we did in some style. We had no intention of buying anything but felt compelled to pop into Chanel, Gucci, and the like just to see what was on offer. I couldn't imagine walking down Bond Street in my condom and entering these shops, but this was somehow a little different. We were now travellers after all.

We popped into Banana Republic, which had fast become David's favourite shop. I recalled that not that

My Travels with Wheely

long ago he used to be so reticent about shopping and had now undergone a change and actually wanted to go shopping, remarkable. Anyway, the salesman in the shop helpfully suggested we purchase an umbrella as they were such a good value. I looked at him and enquired how we were supposed to hold an umbrella as David was pushing me and if I were holding it I'd poke him in the eye. "Oh," he said, "I didn't think of that." It just showed you how thoughtless people could be.

It continued to rain all day until around 17.00, when the sky cleared and the sun came out. We might well be in with a chance of seeing a beautiful sunset tonight. Patience was a virtue; we were indeed rewarded by witnessing the most glorious sunset. I didn't know what it was about sunsets but they certainly bring out the crowds and everyone started talking to their neighbour about how wonderful it was, and it was almost as though we were seeing this strange phenomenon for the very first time. We are the most peculiar of species.

An Australian woman informed me that she has been here for eight days and this was the first sunset here that she had seen. The Hawaiian Islands really were experiencing untypical weather, like the rest of the world. It transpired that she had specifically come here accompanied by her father to go to a wedding, poor things the weather was dreadful, and a number of the guests got food poisoning. She also told me that her thirty-nine-year-old brother had taken his own life in January so her father was understandably taking it very badly. She was a very special lady and I imagined a great comfort to her father in their troubled times.

Nicky Dalladay

E-mails Received

Just read your latest e-mail re NZ and I can honestly say I now feel completely exhausted. Truly pleased you're having a fabulous time but that ferry trip must have been an experience never to be forgotten. Your description was so realistic, I felt a bit seasick just reading it. Carry on having a great time and looking forward to your next missive. J&JW

Really enjoyed your rather terrifying (the ferry) yet humorous rendition of your experiences having just come from NZ. We have had a great trip and we leave for home soon we are excited about seeing family and friends. We will stay in touch; you never know, our paths may cross again. Safe travels and watch those ferries. M&L, Sounds of Silence Dinner at Ayers Rock.

Day Sixty-five

Oh how wonderful, it was not raining, and everywhere looked beautiful. What a difference the sun made. We had booked a trip for today (glad it wasn't yesterday), for a scenic Diamond Head and rainforest tour. This adventure was designed to take in many of the most scenic vistas and natural attractions of Oahu in just a few hours; we enjoyed the panoramic views of Diamond Head, Waikiki, and Honolulu.

The tour was indeed very scenic and beautiful, and the only thing that really ruined it was the tour guide. Luckily for him he was blessed with the power of speech, unluckily for us he didn't know when to stop. Clearly he was unable or perhaps chose to ignore his paying customers and managed to amuse himself by laughing at his own jokes when nobody else did, what a comedian. He really wasn't endearing himself to us at all. He parked the coach at the most ridiculous, inaccessible places for me to get off, and he offered not an iota of assistance. To sum him up, he was a joke. Mental note: *don't tip the prat.*

E-mails Received

Just a swift note to say how very entertained we have been with your adventures, wish we were there. New Zealand sounds amazing and can visualize its beauty through watching the *Lord of the Rings* trilogy. We've more or less been hibernating, waiting for the weather to improve. D&S

Nicky Dalladay

Phew! That ferry crossing was a hairy, scary experience. Glad though that you flew the flag in the time-honoured Brit tradition. For many years, and pre *The Lord of the Rings*, various friends of ours that had travelled to the Southern Hemisphere unilaterally declared NZ to be the most beautiful country on Earth. So now you are in the good ol' U.S. of A! Look forward to update no. 7. No doubt you are like the proverbial Cheshire cats if you have read or heard about events at home…our freeze goes on and on…even the crocuses have only just bloomed when they normally show off in January. Buds on trees are only just about there, while our temperature dials are turned up even higher at night…and all looks set to continue for at least the forthcoming week, still keeping our long johns on too. Just got back from a walk and it feels as if my ears are about to drop off. Look forward to the next instalment. GD

You can always rely on the good old Brits to mention the weather. What is it about us and the weather? It appears to be one of our firm favourites of conversation.

Day Sixty-six

Oops, it was chucking down with rain again, so we get out the condoms — how nice? Today's excursion was a visit to Pearl Harbor and we were both looking forward to this for many reasons. We had all seen countless films depicting the historical moment when the Japanese bombed Pearl Harbor, but somehow there was no substitute for actually being there. After all these years it afforded you the briefest of glimpses and you could only try and imagine just how truly awful it must have been. The film footage shown to us in the Arizona Memorial Centre enabled us to relive the moments in history that were responsible for thrusting America into World War II. It was deeply moving and almost unbelievable that somebody could capture on film the invasion, the total destruction of human life, and the machinery whilst under attack; this was a heart-rending moment.

We were herded out of the cinema in true military fashion onto the navy launch and taken across Pearl Harbor to board the USS *Arizona Memorial*. There was a marble piece etched with all of the names of the crew who had perished on the boat, and it also had the names of those who had subsequently died as it was their wish to be interned with their shipmates. This was a very emotional moment even for the hardest of people.

Then we were taken to the USS *Missouri*. In 1945 this battleship was chosen to be the stage for the signing of

Nicky Dalladay

Japan's Formal Instrument of Surrender. The signing of this document by both the Japanese and the Allied powers brought an end to the world's bloodiest war. It was here that we met two women from Florida who had brought their fathers for their eightieth birthdays to visit Pearl Harbor, a place they had not been back to since they were young men. This was a very significant and personal trip they were on, and a complete surprise as their daughters had arranged it all without their knowledge.

The USS *Missouri* was impossible for me to get around, so I sat somewhere to wait for David. One of the old boys came and sat next to me and told me about his days in the war, where he served on a submarine. I asked him about his tattoos, and he said it was almost obligatory, that everyone got them done the day they signed up, as was taking up smoking, although he said he nearly died trying to inhale a cigarette. They were a smashing bunch of people and a privilege to have met them.

The bus driver for the day was a Hawaiian lady accompanied by two young protégés on their first day in the tourist industry; they evidently needed to put in a lot of hard work before they would be allowed out on their own. Fortunately, the lady was a joy to listen to and was entertaining and informative. She had a fantastic Hawaiian accent and pronounced things in such a specific way it reminded me of Steve Martin's character in the film *The Man with Two Brains*. The names of places were so difficult to pronounce in Hawaii you were almost sure to get it wrong when you attempted to say them.

Back at base, and the condoms could be neatly packed

My Travels with Wheely

away, for at the moment it was only drizzling, and there was nothing much to do there so, we made for Banana Republic again. I would seriously have to rethink my initial thoughts about buying shares in Starbucks. I was obviously being a bit too hasty; Banana Republic shares would have to be added into the equation as well.

Shopping now well and truly completed, we made our tracks toward the hotel. On the way back we passed a market, and I watched someone having her hair braided, which looked a little painful, but I decided I'd like to have it done. I was comforted by the fact that the little girl who had just had it done hadn't burst into tears. Relieved it was obviously not anywhere near as painful as it looked; I opted for a half-head braid. The girl who did it warned me that it would be important to put sunscreen on my now-exposed scalp to prevent burning, she must be having a laugh I thought, *we've hardly seen the sun since we got here.*

Day Sixty-seven
Flight Fourteen

Departure day was here once again as today we would leave Oahu and fly to The Big Island. However, we were dropped at the airport, only to discover it was the wrong terminal. The only way to get to the right terminal was for us to walk, wheel, pull, and push the expanding donkey train whilst dripping in sweat. How delightful we must have looked. Right, we were now at the proper terminal and checked in, and it was utter chaos there. Quite frankly I was amazed that flights managed to arrive and depart from this airport at all. Not sure if David was trying to make me feel better, but he reminded me that we had several more flights to take in the United States, and we collapsed into hysteria at the thought of this.

Eventually, I was brought up to the plane in Wheely, and we took a picture of him in the extending tunnel as he looked somewhat dejected, and for the briefest of moments, I honestly didn't think we'd see him again. On arrival at the Big Island it was with great relief we saw our old and trusted friend Wheely sitting on the tarmac waiting to greet us. I thought, *hold on Wheely, it looks as though you could be in for a long wait.*

The clock moved on in time but we didn't. All the other passengers had long gone, and come to think of it so had most of the crew. It turned out that on this occasion we had to wait an inordinate amount of time to get off, and I

My Travels with Wheely

wondered why. Soon enough, it all became a little clearer, there were only steps to get onto this plane, and no real provisions had been made for the disabled contingent to embark or disembark. We looked out the window to try and establish why we had to wait for so long, and the reason stared us in the face. They were loading another disabled person on to a piece of equipment that can only be described as an "up market" forklift truck.

Poor bloke didn't look to be in particularly good shape and had an entourage of three people carrying various pieces of equipment, no doubt to sustain his life in some way. As an observer and someone who believed passionately in the right to a dignified life as well as death, I wondered if he had considered going to Switzerland, although I realized his life was his own and I did not have the right to decide what he should or should not do with it. I found myself comparing my own situation, and whilst it appeared that I was in a much better shape physically, naturally I wondered if I would end up in the same way.

I couldn't dwell on my feelings as that was not fair to either me or David. Needless to say, they eventually all got boarded and seated, so finally after an hour we could alight. I glanced at "chummy" and smiled at him, but he just glared at me; perhaps it would not be such a good time to mention Switzerland to him.

I was taken down in the same contraption as chummy, experiencing yet another mode of transport to be added to my ever-growing list; what a spoilt girl I was. Now at the carousel to identify our mountain of luggage, no

Nicky Dalladay

worries there; everyone else had departed ages ago; ours was all that was left merrily going around the belt.

We grabbed a taxi to take us to the hotel and just stared out the window, mesmerized by the black volcanic roadside we saw carrying on forever. It was a long road of nothing really, the only thing that broke it up were the white pebbles spelling out names. Where they were carried from I've no idea, but an awful lot of people had made a big effort to do this.

We arrived at the only hotel we'd had to make our own reservation for, so it should be perfect. We had booked an ocean-view room with a walk-in shower. But it was wrong, and we got a shower in a tub. We did have a full ocean view, although somewhat marred by the bright yellow dumper truck in the foreground. We marched back to the reception desk, where we learned of their great surprise that this room did not suit my disabled requirements. Would they ever cotton to the fact that my legs were not capable of lifting themselves up? I realized it was terribly inconvenient of my legs, but that's the way it is. At last, the room had now successfully been changed to the only one available, which was a ground floor, side ocean view of the yellow dumper truck.

Now fully ensconced in our new home for the next few days, the donkey train was dismantled and the contents arranged as appropriate. We ventured from the hotel to see what there was around in terms of entertainment or restaurants; basically there was very little to do in the surrounding area. Our first impression was that it was a strange place with a row of hotels, admittedly

My Travels with Wheely

some distance apart, and a shopping complex with a few restaurants opposite our hotel; it was okay, nothing more, and nothing less. We decided to have lunch at a restaurant where you could sit outside as it was such a beautiful day but in order to smoke you had to go to the other side of the rail so you were not on the restaurant's footprint. Funnily enough, everyone is more than happy to levy a large tax on cigarettes and even to sell them, but the tricky part is trying to find somewhere that you can actually smoke them. That's quite enough of me remonstrating about smoking.

Back to where we were, food, or perhaps I should say that whilst it was called a restaurant it was in fact a burger bar with an extensive choice of burgers and chips but not a lot else. Although they did have a wine list, which was good to know; this meant we didn't have to drink Coke. Having looked at the list we'd love to know how Veuve Clicquot would react to their Champagne being listed as a fizzy wine, and the immortal words sprang into my head again: no taste, and definitely no class.

E-mails Received

A refund of $297.00 has been processed to your credit card due to the inclement weather conditions on your recent ferry sailing. Trust you will find this satisfactory. Ferry Tickets Online.

You must feel as if you have been away forever…and good for you too. It is so wonderful to get your updates, they are so well described that I almost feel I am with you at times…wow, what a boat ride. You seemed to really

Nicky Dalladay

enjoy that experience, I'm not sure I would have been so brave. As you say, sometimes the seriousness of a situation only sinks in once the stiff upper lip isn't required. Well done to you both for preserving the British resolve in such a situation, I'm proud of you. You are really making the most of your time and experiencing so much. It really is wonderful to hear that you are having such an amazing experience. Apart from the campervan it sounds as if everything is living up to your expectations. I can't wait to hear what happens next. Things here just tick over really. Still cold and dark…however as the clocks are going forward soon I am looking forward to lighter nights in the evening so I don't feel such a hermit. I had better get on with some work. It's great to hear from you and keep the updates coming. They really do brighten up an otherwise very dull day. WR

The ferry company rebated the money as promised, and as mentioned previously, I personally would have paid more, it was utterly exhilarating. Inclement weather conditions, pah!

Day Sixty-eight

Finally, the real reason we are here and the lynchpin for this entire trip that I mentioned in the Introduction. The wedding invitation we received back in the summer last year came from a lady called CJ who I met in a work capacity in Luxembourg, and although we had not seen each other for some years, we had kept in touch. David had never met CJ before and obviously neither of us had met her intended, Scott, so we were looking forward to meeting them. I hoped that I'd recognize her and when she met me she wouldn't be taken aback to see me in a wheelchair, although she did know I have MS.

We ambled along to reception to find her room number, and there was a lady talking to the receptionist. I looked at the back of her and said to David I was certain it was her. She turned around with a broad grin on her face. She had recognized me instantly and bounded over to give me a big hug and kiss; it was so good to see her again. She had been busy trying to locate all of her wedding guests and had nearly accounted for all of them. Naturally, she was very anxious about her forthcoming nuptials and told us about the respective hen and stag nights this evening. I worried that David, who didn't know anyone at all, would be reluctant to go on the stag night but he met Scott, who assured David they would not leave without him. We arranged to meet in the bar later when the lads and lasses would go their separate ways.

How exciting! I dressed up and put on a little bit of makeup for the second time this trip. Tonight I was going out with the girls by myself, and this would be the first break that David and I have had from each other for quite some time. I was certain he was looking forward to it as much as I was.

We all met at the appointed time in the bar, and it was wonderful to meet some old faces again. CJ automatically went to push me when a friend of hers said, "No way, it's your night." With that, the larger-than-life Merrill took control and practically ran with me up the road; I could tell she was a terrific girl. We got to the restaurant and settled down for an evening of fun, and I hoped David was having a good time.

At the end of our riotous evening on the town we weaved our way back to the hotel, some a little wobblier than others. I, on the other hand, could get away with murder; my secret was safe with Wheely. No one could tell if I've had a drink or not, pretty useful I'd say, although the slight slurring of words was a bit of a giveaway.

Back at the hotel we met some of the boys who had just returned and we all had several drinks together. There was much to laugh about and it was all very easy, almost as if we'd known everyone for many years. All in all, it was a perfect drunken evening.

E-mail Received

I absolutely love your travelogues; C and I spent six days in NZ eleven years ago (where did they go?). We had a hair-raising journey back from Picton and still laugh about it.

My Travels with Wheely

NZ remains high on my list to return to and your hippy journey has whetted my appetite. It's so fantastic to hear your adventures. Can I edit and publish?! MH

Well my darling, I usually hold people to their promises, never more so than right now.

Day Sixty-nine

Today we looked at what trips were on offer but sadly there were none that were suitable for us on this very dull and rainy day.

What were we going to do? We decided that we could rent a car, and we did just that. Not any old car, but we had chosen to rent a glorious red Mustang convertible for a day. Now we could really let our free spirits come out along with the brilliant sunshine that by some miracle had now emerged. Just how cool was this? With a struggle we managed to get Wheely in the car. You do seem to lose a bit of street cred when trying to shove a wheelchair into a convertible, but oh, what the hell, why should my trusted friend Wheely miss out on this.

At last, we were all aboard the convertible, and, finally we were off, cruising along the roads of "The Big Island." We had managed to tune in to the sound of the 60s on the radio, which was now blaring. The wind was blowing through our hair, well, mine anyway. David was in his element wearing his white T-shirt, jeans, and his beloved Harley Davidson belt that he had bought in Oahu, and his arm was casually hanging out of the window. What a "dude" he was, just loving the experience, I could tell just by looking at his face.

As for me, there was nothing better than feeling the wind in my hair, or perhaps I should say my head as my hair was

My Travels with Wheely

so heavily braided, while breathing the fresh sea air. This was just the best thing to do as it allowed us to explore and see the real beauty of the island, and of course there was no one hurrying you along. We were both just happy travellers singing our way around the island.

Day Seventy

We still had the car for this morning, so we took off in the opposite direction from yesterday and headed toward Kona. It was a splendid day, and we stopped to buy coffee and a roll before finding a wonderful place to sit overlooking the sea. It was the gardens of a church and it occurred to me it would be a rather nice place to be buried at this spot. We savoured the last moments of this beauty and headed back to the hotel we managed to notch up 128 miles before returning our beloved Mustang, it was a brilliant.

Time to get ready now; today was the wedding.

Meeting for drinks in the bar was a jolly good way to commence the proceedings, and we mingled with some of the guests that we had already met. It was really wonderful to see that the majority of people had taken note of the dress code which was casual-nice with a Hawaiian flair. At the appointed time we ventured toward the gardens, which were adjacent to the sea, for the ceremony. As we approached we were each presented with a Hawaiian Lei, a magnificent garland of lemon-coloured flowers, the smell was utterly divine. We all sat and awaited the arrival of the bride. We were not disappointed, she looked fabulous, and her husband-to-be looked adoringly at her. It was a beautiful wedding and we both felt very touched and honoured to have been asked to share this very special day.

My Travels with Wheely

Funnily enough, we were plied with yet more to drink at the reception followed by a sumptuous meal and yet more to drink, as if we needed more. Ah, and then there was the dancing. I was so envious I couldn't participate, but I didn't cry; I really didn't want to ruin what had been a spectacular day. It just reminded me of what once was and that I used to be able-bodied. I merely mentioned to Merrill, who I was sat next to during dinner how much I would love to dance, and before I realized what she was doing she whisked me off to the dance floor. My goodness she was quite mad, did she not realize I couldn't stand, let alone dance? I was right, she was bonkers, and she proceeded in wheeling me around the dance floor. We laughed and laughed until my cheeks hurt.

I am truly lost for words to describe what she did for me; this woman who I had only met days ago did more for me at that time than some people I've known for years; she was indeed extraordinary. David was a little overawed by this episode as I've said to him on previous occasions that sometimes we just needed to be a little more creative, but neither of us knew how, until this moment. He took me for a spin on the dance floor a little later, and while it was certainly not ideal and I would prefer not dance in this way, but as I have little choice in the matter I would go as far to say it was better to experience this than not at all.

"The best and most beautiful things in this world cannot be seen or even heard but must be felt with the heart."

Helen Keller

E-mail Received

I'm absolutely fascinated by the details of your travels. I hope you are going to put them together in a book! Reading the NZ edition coincided with my watching a DVD of New Zealand. I really enjoyed our few hours together in Bangkok. By now you will be experiencing life in USA. I hope the rest of your epic journey is as enjoyable and colourful. MF

Ah, book has been mentioned yet again. I really believe there is a chance.

My Travels with Wheely

The Wedding and the Reason for Travelling

Day Seventy-one
Fourth Helicopter Flight

Thumping heads and an early start, how nice? Actually there was a good reason for getting up so early; we were off on another helicopter flight. The magic just kept on happening.

The trip was a good hour and a half over the many long continuous lava fields of the island, which were quite impressive although not what you would really call pretty. They were quite black and bleak actually, and as a result there was very little here in the way of housing and people.

We flew over a live volcano and saw molten lava, which we were reliably informed by our pilot, was around two thousand degrees. It was the most amazing brilliant red-orange colour, and we all clicked away with our cameras. After all, we'd only ever seen this sort of thing on TV before and not in real life, so of course we were going to go mad on photos. We hovered in valleys, witnessed the landscapes, and felt our cameras sadly would not do this justice, it was just so intense. This was a thoroughly good trip and we were glad we had made the effort to get up so early.

David was packing once more as we got ready to bid a fond farewell before leaving for San Francisco, and I found time to send an e-mail update.

My Travels with Wheely

Seventh E-mail

Aloha from Honolulu, the island of Oahu! Now that our hippy days are well and truly over, we have now become "beach bums." That is to say "Wheely bum" and "dude"! We arrived late on um, er, ah, we think it was Friday, not too sure as we crossed the date line and rather cleverly arrived before we left, way too much for us simple folk to deal with. Not only that but rather than being ahead of the United Kingdom in time we are now behind, although I haven't actually changed my watch. Not that that has helped in the slightest.

Well here we are in downtown Waikiki, part of Hawaii in a hotel that appears to be stuck in a time warp circa 1960s. No, really, it is, believe me. Rather interestingly we have three beds in our room, all of equal size. If only I could jump from bed to bed, that would make David smile!

Anyway, it's good to be back in shorts and T-shirts again. Whilst NZ was warm it was a little on the chilly side; after all, it was autumn.

So it's back to where we are now. We spent the first day walking along by the beach and just enjoying the warmth and taking in the beautiful scenery with Diamond Head point on one side and the Pacific Ocean on the other.

I seemed to have developed a liking for talking to complete strangers and today was no different (mind you I've always done that). There was a lovely elderly Polynesian woman sat in a chair, that's by the by really, it was when she opened her mouth minus several front teeth but she had the most amazing smile and was wearing a magnificent hat. You do

Nicky Dalladay

meet some fabulous people on your travels.

In keeping with the Wheely bum look I had my hair braided. Well, to be more accurate, half a head. The only thing she forgot to tell me was that it would be uncomfortable to sleep with. Ah, the price of being a fashion icon.

David purchased his wedding shirt today, a lovely shirt it is too, if you like that sort of thing. He purchased something else and seems to have got into the buying-something-for-himself mode of late. We were in the Harley Davidson shop, and as I mentioned before our luggage was tight, so instead of buying the actual bike he went for a belt, so please make the appropriate noises when you get your first glance of it. (There's something about men and motor bikes when they get past age fifty).

Talking of back in shorts, the DallAwayDays purchased some rather fetching his and hers combat shorts. Or should I say his and his? Yes I've grown to such proportions that it was necessary to buy men's shorts; "dude" got quite excited as I tried on the same waist size as him saying that we could swap because they are different colours. Imagine his face when I had to go up a size, but then he thought about it and said he would wear them after they'd been washed to stretch them for me.

Ah, and then there was the rain. It lashed down all day, and we felt we had to buy something to keep us dry, so we went to the ABC store and purchased two very fetching rain cloaks. Well to say we looked like a couple of condoms walking down the street is no word of a lie; we looked truly silly, but hey, we were dry. You will not miss out on this latest

My Travels with Wheely

fashion faux pas. No doubt they will come in very useful in downtown Loughton and you can borrow them.

Whilst I think of it, it'll be a miracle if we don't arrive home calling everyone "guys," since we have been greeted like that since Oz. You have been warned.

We went on a lovely tour of Diamond Head Point, scenic routes, and the rainforest, and all the sights were gorgeous. The only downside was the tour guide who obviously fancied himself as Robin Williams in *Good Morning Vietnam*, and if ever you felt you wanted to punch somebody this was indeed the moment. We also went to visit Pearl Harbor, which was hugely emotional; the film footage was amazing, quite unbelievable that someone could take this whilst under attack. The memorial site was also very moving as it had all the names of those who died on the USS *Arizona,* as well as those that survived and had their remains buried with their shipmates; very touching.

Tonight we dined out at the Royal Hawaiian Hotel, where absolutely everything was pink. All that was consumed this evening was Mai Tais and nachos. God, he really knows how to show a girl a good time.

Now what is really associated with Hawaii is the surfing. Well, what a big fat con that is. There were no waves even half the height we saw on the ferry (see e-mail no. 6). Surfing is an odd way to spend your time. You just hang around for hours, or so it seems, for something half decent, and then you have to paddle back again. It was an awful lot of hard work for what appeared to be very little reward.

We have now left Oahu and in the main, the miserable

Nicky Dalladay

weather warm but cloudy and arrived on The Big Island, where at present the weather is equally miserable but warm.

Yes The Big Island and the wedding, the real reason for us travelling. The hotel seems to be undergoing extensive renovation and as such a few dumper trucks are in view. We did our usual room-changing routine, since our fourth-floor ocean view room with a, wait for it, arghhh, another bath with a shower in it had to be swapped with a side view of the aforementioned dumper truck.

The weather has not improved that much — very warm and cloudy — but at least no rain (i.e. no condoms either).

We tried to book some tours but found nothing suitable, so we rented a car, a Ford Mustang convertible. Oh boy, what a great day we had cruising the lava fields with wind blowing through my half a head of braided hair — not applicable to David of course. But hey, he was driving with an arm hanging out the window, his shades on, and the 60s music on the radio blaring out, well, we just rocked, man.

We both had great fun on our respective hen & stag dos and we all ended up meeting in the bar after to finish the evening's drinking session, and what a lovely bunch of people we met.

The wedding was beautiful; a more gorgeous setting you could not ask for. All guests were given a Lei (we could make comments but best not go there), and the fragrant smell in the air was wonderful. As requested the dress code was Hawaiian casual, all the shirts were incredible, needless to say, and the bride looked stunning. We chatted, drank,

My Travels with Wheely

and danced the night away. When I say danced, Wheely and I joined in too, which was indeed a very special moment.

We got up at the crack of dawn to go on yet another helicopter ride, and we'll be applying for a license before you know it. This was a pretty spectacular one and lasted for an hour and half. We traversed the lava fields; saw molten lava bubbling in one of the live volcanoes, lava going into the sea and smouldering and emitting sulphur/steam. We also saw a whale breaching out at sea. As if that's not enough we flew into deep valleys, and it was indeed an exceptional flight.

Well, readers, we have now done Hawaii, and David is about to start cramming things into the suitcase again. Where's Mary bloody Poppins when you need her?

Love to everyone
DallAwayDays
xxxx

Nicky Dalladay

Off to see Molten Lava

Day Seventy-two
Flight Fifteen, San Francisco

What utter chaos at Kona airport. It was chucking down with rain and what looked like a really sweet open air airport on arrival in the balmy Hawaiian sun now resembled a quagmire. There was hardly any cover, and most of us looked like drowned rats. The woman who was supposed to be boarding us on the plane lost it completely and apparently was unable to cope with either the people or the deluge of rain. Oh dear, her score was not looking as though it was going to be very good, although the rain would of course be taken into consideration.

One minute she was telling David and me to come forward for boarding and the next she was saying there's no one to board people in wheelchairs, can I walk? Naturally, there was a negative reply so we were then asked to move out the way for able-bodied passengers to proceed with boarding. After an age it now appeared that everyone had boarded, apart from us. We were then hurriedly ushered to go to the far end of the plane to be boarded at the rear end. Just an incy wincy minute detail barely worth mentioning, but nonetheless, I felt should be pointed out: our seats were actually in row one in the front of the airplane.

So now what awaited us was a cleaning truck to lift me up to the aircraft door, and the only problem, which was quite significant, was the girl trying to operate it just didn't know how it worked. She said rather embarrassedly

Nicky Dalladay

she had only started this job last week. I give up. After much pushing of knobs and lever pulling, finally we managed to board the plane, hooray. The only problem that remained was now I had to be manoeuvred from the very back to the front on the most ridiculous aisle chair, with no wheels. We were soaking wet, as were our bags and everything we were carrying, the plane was full, and the passenger's bodies seemed to spill over into the aisles, so this was not going to be easy.

To assist our passage I felt compelled to keep saying, "Excuse us, drop-dead-gorgeous woman coming through." It had the desired effect; they moved with a grunt or two. Oddly enough, we were late taking off, couldn't think why, it must have been the wrong type of rain. Well done, Kona Airport, we thought you won hands down in being the worst airport we'd ever had the misfortune to fly to and from. By the way, I awarded the airport and staff zero. It should really have been worse but I did take the rain into consideration, as promised.

We arrived in San Francisco, and the weather had seemed to follow us there, and the rain continued to fall from the big black clouds. We picked up a taxi and were taken to the hotel. *Very smart,* we both thought and reckoned this time we had done extremely well. We were checked in, and one handicapped room was ready and waiting for us. It struck me as rather odd that in some countries I was considered disabled, which sort of meant to me that I was able but my body just didn't function very well. Whilst in some other countries I was handicapped, which could conjure up pictures of my hands being capped and they didn't exist, which was really not the

My Travels with Wheely

case. Granted they were quite useless, but nevertheless, I did have them.

Anyway, back to the point, we were shown to our allegedly handicapped room. I didn't believe it as once again the shower was in a tub, or a bath to the rest of us. If this room was supposedly designed specifically for the handicapped, I could no more get into the tub than I could climb up the north face of the Eiger. Someone must surely be having a laugh?

Today had not been a good day; my health and my spirits remained good and positive but — and it is a big but — sadly, Wheely had evidently encountered further damage courtesy of the airline. For the second time the airlines had demonstrated their lack of respect of other people's property, and we both felt very sorry for him. I noted, with cynicism creeping into my head, that this had to be a perfect end to a perfect day. Exasperated, it was late and we were tired, so we went to sleep. We would try and deal with the shower in the morning.

E-mails Received

Hi, travellers. Hope you're enjoying yourselves. All fun here: we're blue this time, M had a baby boy, no name yet! C&PF

Dear DallAwayDays, Just came back from holiday with G. We went to a wedding in Germany (seems to be the year of the weddings) we rented a car for a few days to go hiking in the mountains north of Italy. It was fabulous and very relaxing. My face even saw a few sun rays… rather rare for me. Wedding organization is moving on

Nicky Dalladay

which is great. Looking forward to you two coming back as I am really missing your company. MK

I don't think you should come home, Just keep travelling because we'll miss your adventurous e-mails too much when they stop. It all sounds so amazing, especially the wedding. Lots of rain here, at last and no complaints, but the gales have nearly blown the doors off their hinges. C&NB

Another life has entered the world and now weddings with one for us to look forward to in Germany, but right now, I feel as though I just want to travel forever.

Day Seventy-three

The sun was now but a distant memory. The rain lashed down, although luckily for us, we had our trusty condoms to help keep us dry. By the way, the shower situation was resolved by them putting a plastic garden chair in the tub. You had to admire their ingenuity under the circumstances as it was the best they could do.

Outside the hotel for a morning smoke whilst David was in the shower, I found I was doing what comes naturally to me, engaging in conversation with a fellow smoker. He introduced himself as Stuart and told me that he lived in Toronto and was with his lady friend, who lived in Seattle. They had in fact met some years ago whilst on holiday after the deaths of their respective spouses. They enjoyed each other's company so much that they vowed to meet up regularly on holiday. Each of them had too much history to give up where they both lived, so they settled for meeting each other for holidays. Clearly they adored one another and would continue to do what suited them both. It was a lovely story.

With yesterday now firmly behind us we walked toward the piers and went in search of brunch. We ordered pancakes and bacon, thinking it would be a light snack. Across the other side of the pond, food has an altogether different meaning. I seemed to get the idea here that the more you could shovel down your gullet, the better. When I uttered the immortal words light

Nicky Dalladay

snack, I genuinely meant it; well it just showed how wrong you could be, and this "Desperate Dan" pile of pancakes twelve inches in diameter and six inches high, arrived. We were never going to wade our way through that and sure enough we didn't.

I found myself being guilty of eavesdropping on other diners' conversation. Some might have said it was nosy, and I would say it wasn't, but I was merely intrigued. I heard the waitress take an order from a diner who wanted eggs, and did they want them over, over-easy or sunny-side up? I also understood that the humble boiled egg didn't exist here; apparently, they didn't have egg cups, so if you wanted a boiled egg you actually received a poached egg; thank god I went for the pancakes else we would have been there for the entire day. This incident served to remind me that whilst we all spoke English, we clearly didn't speak the same language.

Feeling somewhat full we waddled out the door and decided to try and take a tram. So far so good; there was a slope and we managed to get to the platform. We hailed the tram and got short shrift from the driver as we appeared to be standing in the wrong place. Well excuse us, how in the hell did we know? Once on the tram, he didn't charge us, maybe he felt bad. We got off at Union Square and had a little mooch around the shops namely Tiffany and Baccarat. We decided to stroll back to the hotel to make the most of it not raining for the time being.

Back at the hotel we thought about where to go for dinner and we chose an Italian restaurant as it looked so

My Travels with Wheely

stunning from the outside. It was a great shame it didn't quite live up to expectation; it was truly awful.

E-mails Received

Your e-mails are heaven and a laugh. I think they should be bound into a volume with all your holiday pictures, I'd buy a copy. Thank god the school holidays are imminent, I'm ready to drop. Either that or kill one of the testosterone ridden little sods. Have a brilliant rest of the time. JB

Sounds like you're having a fantastic trip. I'm very jealous at this end as I sit by the ice rink at Broadgate in the rain. The regular e-mail brings a smile and C and I are looking forward to a marathon two-hour slideshow when we get together on your return if, of course, you're silly enough to come back at all. Looking forward to the next missive. JF

Thanks, D-days, sounds like you're having an amazing time. Makes my three-day trip last week to Portugal seem like a trip to Sainsbury's. From the sound of it, I am surprised that you didn't bump into Steve McGarrett during your Hawaii trip. I trust you have taken plenty of photos of the pink restaurant at the Royal Hawaiian Hotel, which I would love to see. Can fully appreciate your desire to punch the Robin Williams sound-alike, I would be next in the queue I can assure you to punch him, not to be punched! Really enjoying your reports, it sounds as if you are doing things in real style and having a fantastic time. RA

We have been reading your messages in awe. May you

Nicky Dalladay

both continue to have a spectacularly wonderful time as you travel. M&AMN

Yet again another fantastic update of your travels which are very much enjoyed and they break up another mundane day in the office. What a fantastic time you are both having. You are doing so much and really making the most of your trip, which is great to hear. Where next? Tonight is our colleagues leaving drink. Your message has been written into his card and will be read out. It is hard to believe that he won't be here next week he is part of the furniture.

I'm desperately trying to think of something interesting and funny to tell you, oh just thought of something. Had lunch with the girls yesterday and one of them was wearing a floaty skirt that caught in the wind as we left the office, it reminded me of an incident when a temp who came back from the ladies with her skirt in her knickers. I emailed her to discretely let her know and she jumped up and screamed, alerting the whole office who previously hadn't spotted it, to her dilemma. Of course we all laughed about this during lunch. We all said how important it is to make a second check before leaving the loos especially if you are wearing a floaty skirt.

Later, the two old soaks had one for the road. One of them came out of the loo, walked back to her seat and realized that people were sniggering. Would you believe it...skirt in knickers! She said that she wasn't wearing her finest either...but at least it wasn't a thong! Anyway, I hope I leave you laughing helplessly...Miss you and look forward to seeing you when you are back. Keep having a

My Travels with Wheely

fantastic time and keep making the most of every day it makes for wonderful reading. WR

Your e-mail certainly did make me laugh. It reminds me of what fun I used to have when going out for a drink with my girlfriends at work. Happy days.

Day Seventy-four

We both needed to rush to the bathroom with our upset stomachs — or more accurately, our bottoms — I'll spare the details, but what a lovely way to start the day. Not to be put off by our delicate lower halves, I thought that Italian wasn't up to much; we made our way to pick up our pre-booked tickets for our trip to Alcatraz Island. We boarded the ferry to cross to the island; the Rock was very impressive to look at.

Yet another milestone was about to be accomplished. We had seen the film and now were actually here and didn't quite believe it; it was about time that we pinched ourselves and duly did just that. Once off the ferry, we were herded to a courtyard to hear the entire list of do's and don'ts whilst on the island, and naturally there were way more don'ts than do's. One could be forgiven for thinking we were convicts by the way they spoke to us. We were ushered toward a trolley vehicle again, this one rather reminiscent of the TV programme *The Prisoner.*

Number five, Alcatraz prison rules and regulations, 1934: "You are entitled to food, clothing, shelter, and medical attention. Anything else you get is a privilege."

This rule was one of the realities of life inside the walls of the U.S. Federal Penitentiary, Alcatraz Island. The subject of many movies and books, Alcatraz has become a symbol of America's dark side. From fiction rather

My Travels with Wheely

than fact, there are stories of the prison and of some of the men who lived in the cells, including Al "Scarface" Capone and Robert Stroud, the "Birdman of Alcatraz." The truth of Alcatraz has often been overlooked and lost in the fog of its myths.

Bearing in mind that today did not start very well, this turned out to be the mother of all days and just got worse. Many a man had been broken by Alcatraz, but I never thought that the Rock would be the demise of my friend Wheely.

We were just shown one of the prisoners' cells. David took some photographs, and the new camera we had purchased in Cairns died. *Oh well*, we thought, we could always buy another one — was that déjà vu? Then we were taken completely by surprise. Without warning my backside virtually ended up on the floor, and the crossbar that held the seat in place finally snapped. The wheels were splayed out so it was not dissimilar to a wheelchair designed for the use of paraplegics for sporting activities.

It was an immensely sad moment; we had become very attached to an inanimate object, my travelling companion, Wheely. We had been served so well by him on our travels and I reflected that it was a great shame that we were now in this position. I was reminded yet again that it just showed that people had so little respect for your property; I was at a loss without Wheely.

The guys at Alcatraz were indeed very helpful and produced an old office chair and sat me on it; now out of

Nicky Dalladay

my wheelchair they tried very hard to put Wheely back together. Whatever they were able to achieve with the limited equipment available to them was only ever going to be a temporary measure, the damage was so great. They found wire and duct tape to patch poor Wheely up so at least we could get back to the mainland. Consequently, as I'm sure you will have gathered, we didn't see a lot of Alcatraz. We managed to have a quick whirlwind tour, purchased a collection of twelve postcards with images of Alcatraz, Federal Penitentiary from 1934 to 1963, and at least we would have some evidence of having been there.

Then I lost it completely.

It was so full of people; I just didn't want to be surrounded by them. I had an overwhelming feeling of claustrophobia and had to get out *now*. When you're trapped in a wheelchair and have a lot of people standing around towering above you, they just don't seem to see you. I am a person.

At that precise moment I felt as if I didn't even exist. My brain was screaming with rage and frustration. Was there really nobody who could help me? In reality there wasn't, and from where I was I could only see a bleak existence. I had since left my previous life as a gregarious young woman and was now somewhere I really didn't want to be.

The feeling that I had was one of terror; it was horrible, and I felt so worthless, helpless, and inadequate. Unable to get out of there by myself and away from the situation

My Travels with Wheely

I found so distressing, David took me outside to try and calm me down.

The rain was back with a vengeance, and it was chucking down. One of the nice chaps came out to see me and said, "Please come back in," but I didn't want to, I couldn't bear to feel hemmed in again. My mouth emitted a mixture of crying, wailing, and screaming, so much that I couldn't speak. I was finding it hard to breathe, my body was convulsing the more I cried, and I was frightened. We were soaked through, but that paled into insignificance. The nice chap disappeared to get a bottle of water to try to comfort me.

Sometime later, soaking wet but a little more composed, we made our way back to the ferry to travel back to the mainland. On the boat, we met a really nice man who told us that he was a national park worker and had worked on the island for about ten years. He informed us there was little money spent on the island to maintain it. The very limited amount that we had managed to see supported his claim; it had been apparent it looked very run down and had been allowed to go to rack and ruin, which was a great shame they hadn't treasured this part of history, but then I supposed that was America for you.

We dripped our way back to the hotel and the concierge helped phone around in search of a wheelchair supplier. Naturally, wheelchair shops were not in abundance, and even if we were at home it would still have been hard to find somewhere. Lady luck was on our side. Having searched their equivalent of our yellow pages they found one that was open until six; we were both amazed and

Nicky Dalladay

delighted. However, time was not really on our side, and we had to hotfoot it across the other side of town. The hotel hailed a cab for us. Bearing in mind that the day hadn't got off to a very good start and it had only got worse, which was a huge understatement, we now found ourselves being entertained by the taxi driver. The taxi ride was a brilliant experience, not one to be missed, and as we went up and down the streets of San Francisco, it resembled something from a film. When you have experienced such a journey it puts *The Streets of San Francisco* into perspective, and it became a reality. It was so simple; a taxi ride meant that our spirits had been lifted, thank god for that. To coin a phrase, this was an awesome experience.

Finally, we got to the wheelchair shop and purchased a second-hand wheelchair to enable us to continue our travels. We eventually got back to the hotel and went to eat in another Italian restaurant; the experience of the night before was certainly not going to put us off. The restaurant was part of the hotel, the food was lovely, and with good service. It had just been the most foul of days, and we wanted it to end on a good note.

My Travels with Wheely

Eighth E-mail
Disaster Strikes on Alcatraz

We went, as every good tourist must, to visit "the Rock," the place that has broken many a strong character. We have to report with great sadness that, having endured mistreatment and abuse from the likes of Quantas and United Airlines, our trusted and faithful Wheely has suffered irreversible and fatal damage. We are deeply saddened by this unfortunate consequence of Wheely's gung-ho attitude of transporting Nicky to *all* places she has wished to go. We are comforted only by the fact that Wheely tackled and conquered terrain that many apparently stronger vehicles would balk at. He will forever be in our memories and in San Francisco!

DallAwayDays
Minus One

Day Seventy-five

We had both really been looking forward to San Francisco, and for the reasons stated, we didn't see the very best of it. With the bad luck we had encountered we did at least manage to see a fraction of the glorious sights. The weather was diabolical, which seemed to us rather fitting, given the circumstances we found ourselves in.

Our dreams were of doing a seaplane tour, a Golden Gate tour, a champagne flight, a city tour, or even Yosemite National Park. The options were endless there was so much to do, but this, sadly, was never to be, and they would have to remain dreams.

This part of our journey proved to be quite a washout, as not a lot had been done in San Francisco, all of our attention had understandably been on the wheelchair. David removed all the duct tape and wire in order to take pictures for insurance purposes. We would have to leave poor Wheely here as his final resting place and would have to continue without him. He would remain in San Francisco when we departed for Las Vegas.

This took the entire morning and we didn't get out of the hotel until after lunch. Guess what? It was raining. We located somewhere to buy another new camera — just how many cameras are required for a trip? We had three thus far plus a disposable camera and an underwater camera. That would make us quite heavy on the camera side.

My Travels with Wheely

Talking of heavy, "Mrs. Lardarse," me, found that her trousers were becoming a little too tight for comfort and for David zipping them up. So to add to the list of cappuccinos and muffins, I could now include chips; I was now paying the price for my overindulgence. We also had to find a jean shop, practical as ever, I thought it may be a good idea whilst we were there and going through this process that we might just as well buy two sizes up, so to eliminate this becoming a problem again. Only joking. Mental note: *eat fewer chips.*

With shopping now done, a new camera and a new larger pair of jeans, we could continue on our way. We walked along by the piers, as our main aim was to get some fresh air. The highlight today was to experience having dinner at a true American diner, and we found a very beautiful place with a distinctive 1930s style, a period I adore. The food was sublime and to die for, and it was the first time we had three courses. Luckily I had just bought a new pair of jeans. I must say it was all gorgeous and it was the first good meal we had in America, and considering we had been here for some weeks, that in itself was quite poor.

Day Seventy-six
Flight Sixteen

All of a sudden we found that our flight from San Francisco to Las Vegas would incur an excess baggage charge. We were not entirely sure how this had happened, because after all, we were travelling "light." Perhaps it was because of my epic proportions?

We left good old San Francisco in cloudy weather and arrived in Las Vegas. It was boiling hot and the contrast couldn't have been more apparent. As we walked through Las Vegas Airport it was obvious we were in the gambling city of the universe. There was an enormous amount of one-armed bandits, and every one of them had somebody putting money into their greedy little slots. Strangely enough, it also appeared to be the only place in the USA where you were allowed to smoke. Consequently, the airport was in a complete haze, fantastic. I did find myself questioning their morals, as it was evidently deeply frowned upon in the rest of the USA, yet here it was perfectly all right to smoke. How bizarre was that?

On our journey from the airport to our hotel we noticed it was very glitzy, bright, loud, brash, and to be honest, exactly how we imagined it should be. Las Vegas looked as though it was a really vibrant and a fun place to be; in fact, it was a real eclectic mix of just about everything. We were both absolutely staggered by the enormity of the Strip; the sheer size of the hotels was

My Travels with Wheely

something we had never seen before, and it all made us feel rather small. The main road that crossed over the Strip had roughly six lanes of traffic either way, making the M25 back home look rather pathetic.

We were dropped off at our hotel, the Luxor. Had somebody changed our itinerary without our knowledge? It looked as though we had suddenly been transported to Egypt. Not only was it enormous, but there was a very large sphinx outside, and the hotel itself resembled a pyramid. Being blunt, it was gaudy and trashy but somehow well suited to the surrounding area. Once inside, we discovered that it was not in the least bit personal. There were queues of people trying to check in, and it reminded me of the supermarkets at home where there were always banks of cashiers and lengthy queues. It turned out that it wasn't so bad though. I had just caught sight of a Starbucks.

Eventually we got to our room and David opened the suitcase to discover a notice from the airline stating that our case had been opened and inspected. For a moment, I hoped that there was nothing untoward packed in the bag, and much to my relief there wasn't, just our dirty underwear, so I just chuckled.

We went for a stroll to look at our surrounding area. It was just like a very big version of toy town, I guessed it must be like visiting Disneyland, I didn't know I had never been, suffice it to say it was out of the ordinary. It was larger than life; everything was so huge and so much money had been invested in this one area. There was an enormous Statue of Liberty, an equally large Eiffel tower, the MGM studio, and countless other famous buildings.

I was vaguely amused to see that Las Vegas attracted a lot of people in wheelchairs. It did seem an extraordinary place to see them. I have made mention of this for the simple reason that since we had been travelling I had actually seen very few people in wheelchairs; perhaps it was just that Las Vegas was very wheelchair friendly.

We decided that we must visit one of the many casinos just so we could say we had experienced them. Positioned by a table we were as ready as we'd ever be, but the pair of us proved to be completely useless. We tried to work out what you were supposed to do on the various gaming tables, to no avail. Don't get me wrong, I like spending money, but I am not a big fan of gambling, so with this in mind we headed for the one-armed bandits. We had no wish to part with serious amounts of money and settled for gambling with $1.50, and a couple of seconds later we were poorer to the tune of $1.50. I deduced that there was not much chance of us being invited to the "high rollers" club.

We wandered through the casino and came across the wedding chapel situated right next to a Pizza Hut, which tickled us. *Only in America could you find this,* we thought. The chapel actually looked quite inviting but was not somewhere I could ever imagine getting married. Seconds later we saw a bride and groom in full wedding regalia feeding the slot machines. Nice?

The only reason for coming to Las Vegas in the first

My Travels with Wheely

place was because we wanted to go to the Grand Canyon. We were not disappointed with Las Vegas and thought it lived up to what it offered, and we were sure there was nowhere else quite like it in the World.

Day Seventy-seven
Light Aircraft Flight

We were picked up from the lobby of our hotel first thing in the morning and taken to a small airport to be greeted by a representative of Scenic Airlines for a sunrise tour in the Grand Canyon. It was very odd, we were now completely taking things in our stride, as we had become accustomed to seeing such spectacular sights; we were almost taking it for granted. That was so wrong of me to feel that way, as I above everybody should know by now that you can take nothing in life for granted, and how dare I feel like this.

The plane was boarded to commence our journey to the Grand Canyon; the flight over the canyon was breathtaking, the emerging colours reminiscent of the sand-filled test tubes you could buy from the beach when I was a child. It was very hard to put into words what we saw, and I understand there is no landscape on Earth that is as surprising to the observer as the vast yet intricate face of the Grand Canyon. Over several million years the Colorado River carved an immense chasm through this arid land. The layers of rock exposed in the canyon walls provide snapshots of the geologic events that shaped the American Southwest.

As we flew over, the pilot pointed out the various plateaus, and of course the Hoover Dam. We were treated to some of the most spectacular panoramic views of this amazing place. There were about eight people on the plane and everybody was continuously taking pictures in the hope they would

My Travels with Wheely

at least get one or two good ones. The flight's duration was about one hour. Imagine how many pictures must have been taken. It was a lovely day and we definitely saw the canyon in all its glory and at its best.

We were taken to our accommodation, and David left me to check out our room. He came back and informed me that once more we were faced with a classic: the shower was in a tub, argh. I just didn't understand how, in a civilized country, we continued to encounter such difficulties in getting a walk-in shower. I was frustrated and furious that we could not achieve what I believed to be a very simple request. Daily I was being made aware that nobody really understood the needs of a disabled person, particularly when she suffered from a degenerative condition resulting in the loss of strength and didn't have any core stability. I found it hard to believe that I was the only disabled person who had ever travelled who was continuously faced with this problem. Now it dawned on me, and the realization sank in as I fully understood why I saw so few people on our travels in wheelchairs. I felt as though we weren't welcome. Strong stuff, I know, but that was how I was made to feel at that exact moment.

We were unable to change room this time so we changed hotel instead. Just as well really, since it was less than glamorous, and that's me being polite. Our bus driver went above and beyond the call of duty to get us in somewhere else and was very helpful; he located a hotel with a bedroom that had a walk-in shower, which was perfect. It just showed you what could be done. It's necessary to stand your ground, but it shouldn't have to be like that.

Nicky Dalladay

We would have to see what was on the schedule for tomorrow. As it stood, it was a little confusing but we felt confident all would be revealed in due course, no doubt.

Indeed it was. A note was shoved under our door.

E-mails Received

RIP Wheely. LA

Oh no! What are you going to do? Hope you have been able to find a suitable replacement. How very sad losing such a good mate. N&CB et al.

Day Seventy-eight
Light Aircraft Flight

We set the alarm for 04.30 in the morning as we were due to see the sunrise at the Grand Canyon. We were being picked up at 05.20, so we were ready and waiting at the appointed time; so far so good. The plan fell somewhat short when the guide arrived later than she should have. She had in fact overslept and eventually pitched up at 05.30. *Don't mind us, love,* we thought. We had flown more than halfway around the world to see the sunrise.

With no word of apology for her tardiness she informed us that we still had to pick up twelve other people. *Terrific,* we thought, *would the sun actually wait for us to arrive before it rose?* No, it wouldn't. We made haste, well she doodled along, to go and pick up the other twelve people, only to discover they had gone. They had evidently got bored waiting and made their own way to see the sunrise.

Off the bus we hurried to the viewing platform to watch the sunrise, but yes, we missed it, we were too late. Even though we were late we were still able to appreciate the beauty of the Grand Canyon and were fixated by the sheer magnificence. We sat and watched the changing play of light and shadows, which was indeed an inspiring view, a very humbling experience. The sun had risen a fair way and it was freezing cold. We had never known anything like it, yet more evidence that she-who-thought-she-had-packed-everything hadn't. David was cold through to the

Nicky Dalladay

bone; he was very uncomfortable.

We went back to the hotel for a hot cup of coffee and breakfast before being picked up again to board another light aircraft to be taken to Monument Valley. David particularly wanted to visit Monument Valley for the very reason that during his youth he had watched many western films made by John Ford, and of course starring the late, great, one and only John Wayne. In many ways you could say this experience was his fantasy that had now become a reality and was yet another dream fulfilled. I pinched David on his behalf.

The valley was gorgeous and stunning, the Earth a brilliant red colour, and the monoliths nothing short of majestic. Behold, it was yet another awe-inspiring sight. They are remnants of a high plateau and have naturally formed over the last millions of years, indeed one of the wonders of the natural world.

Our new camera, that was to say our third camera, used rechargeable batteries, but I had stupidly forgotten to put the extra ones in my bag. The batteries we had run out so quickly, David had to go in search of more, and luckily he found some.

Although English was our native tongue, we seemed to be on a tour full of Japanese people, and the tour guide was a Japanese woman who either refused to speak English or couldn't, we were unsure. Anyway, she successfully confused us and a French couple about the lunch arrangements. We both inadvertently missed lunch as I opted to have a cigarette, by which time the lunch was over, supporting my

My Travels with Wheely

theory in the USA your body was merely a repository for food. The French people informed me it was something like gruel and we had not really missed anything. Onward and we all load back on to the open top bus for more breathtaking views.

The Japanese woman was really doing her hardest to irritate me. Call it PMT or whatever you like, I actually fell out with her. I had what can only be described as a sense of humour failure, and I pointed out to her that she did in fact have English-speaking people on the tour and she should be more courteous. Being adults we at least managed to make it up and were quite civil to each other for the rest of the day, and she offered to take a picture of David and me at a rather spectacular point.

After the tour, Daniel our coach driver, was responsible for taking us back to the hotel when he suddenly asked what was wrong with me, so I told him. He said that he thought it was MS and revealed his "mom" had it as well and was bedridden. She also weighed twenty stone. I couldn't help but wonder if that was the reason she was in bed, and in reality I should not be casting aspersions as it was none of my business.

Our itinerary was indeed very confusing as we were supposed to visit Bryce Canyon, but for some reason that never became clear to us it was cancelled, which was another thing to add to our list to sort out at home. I made it sound as though the list was enormous, but it wasn't. It was a wheelchair, two cameras, and Bryce Canyon. Not really very much when you considered how long we had been away. David packed our suitcase, as tomorrow

Nicky Dalladay

morning we would be on a flight to take us back to Las Vegas.

E-mails Received

Oh dear, oh dear…! I was playing bridge last night with friends, and we all drank a toast to "Wheely." Hopefully you gave him a decent send-off: RIP. Well, now we're in April, I suppose you're on the home stretch, no doubt with very mixed feelings: we'll all have to make sure that there are lots of parties when you get back so that you don't both fall into a decline! VM

Dear Remaining DallAwayDays, Devastated to hear of your loss! But thrilled as always to hear your upbeat version of the amazing things you've been up to. LE

We have so far received news of births, marriages; the only remaining one to go of course was the death section, Wheely. It was so heart-warming to read that many people had embraced Wheely as much as we had. He would indeed hold a very special place in our hearts.

My Travels with Wheely

Monument Valley

Day Seventy-nine
Light Aircraft Flight

Another dawn meant another day and of course another light aircraft flight back to Las Vegas, over the vast landscape of the Grand Canyon, breathtaking. Yes we did have a few problems, but they were by no means enough to take away from us the sights we had seen, and we pinched each other.

We disembarked the light aircraft and went in search of our transfer, only to find that the bus that was due to take us back to downtown Las Vegas had broken down. It transpired that our charming man who picked us up was nothing like charming; in fact, I seemed to recall that he was called "Mr. Stroppy," aptly named by my good self, of course. After much huffing and puffing the bus was fixed and we could board it. That wasn't good enough for Mr. Stroppy. Oh no, he had clearly decided he was going to continue being as miserable as possible and proceeded to sigh continuously until he dropped us off at our hotel. He clearly was having a very bad day. I think he was expecting a tip from us but any tip I would give him would be to cheer up.

We had been delivered by Mr. Stroppy to the Bellagio Hotel. One wondered how it was possible that two hotels on the Strip could be so extreme; this hotel was just gorgeous. Granted it was indeed big, flashy, and opulent but streets ahead of the last one we stayed in, and it was

My Travels with Wheely

just beautiful. We hadn't even gone further than the check-in desk where the ceiling was decked with the most fabulous ornate glass flowers. The girls who checked us in were very welcoming, wore the most glamorous outfits, and were surrounded by fresh flowers.

En route to our bedroom we passed the hotel shopping arcade. They weren't just any old shops. There was Chanel, Dior, Giorgio Armani, Prada, Yves St. Laurent, and my beloved Tiffany and Co. I wondered why David had suddenly increased his speed. I felt he thought I might miraculously jump out of the wheelchair and run into the shops, if only I could. *Phew,* thought David, he had managed to run past the shops so quickly he really believed I hadn't noticed them; ah but I've got news for you, I had.

We had been blessed once again with the most beautiful weather, so we decided to go for a walk; this was new territory as this was the other end of the Strip. We walked to Caeser's Palace because we felt we should as it was very famous and not to go there would be a great shame. In the foyer we were rewarded by seeing Elton John's red tour piano on display. He was obviously due to play there soon, but sadly, we would not be there.

Las Vegas was so full of life, and the tourists were very colourfully dressed. There was something about the sunshine that made people wear the most ridiculous clothes, whereas in winter most of us are covered up well. Yet when the sun comes out we are under the misapprehension that our bodies are really quite nice, so we display every bit of flesh possible; bad move.

Nicky Dalladay

Nearly back at our hotel where we saw the most fantastic fountain displays. The Bellagio lakefront comes to life with a mesmerizing ballet of water choreographed to the music of such artists as Luciano Pavarotti and Frank Sinatra. The displays are every half an hour or so and each time was a different piece of music and a different water display. The first time I saw this I was very emotional. I had never seen anything quite so beautiful in my life and the fact a fountain had the ability to make you cry said enough.

Our bedroom was lovely and the windows were full size, which gave us a panoramic view of the whole of Vegas. I don't think either of us realized just how vast this place was. When you think of Las Vegas you really only think of the Strip, and no consideration is really given to the surrounding area. For all the people who work there, of course they must live somewhere and there would clearly have to be a lot of infrastructure in place to ensure the Strip was what it was.

Our time here was drawing to a close, and we now realized we only had a couple of weeks left. David gets all of our things together and stuffs them in the case; a proper repack would have to be done, but not just now. Tonight we had just ordered room service. It was early evening but we had to depart first thing tomorrow morning for Toronto.

After dinner we went for a walk and found ourselves in one of the many shopping malls situated underneath the hotels. The malls were so huge and extremely well thought out, and even as a person who doesn't particularly

My Travels with Wheely

enjoy mass shopping found myself admiring them.

We stopped for the last time to watch the fountains, and each display seemed to be more spectacular than the last.

E-mails Received

That was sad news to come into on a Monday morning. I hope Wheely had a decent send off. Hopefully you have a suitable replacement for the duration of your travels. I loved San Francisco and apart from the sad Wheely news, I hope you had a good time there. Our colleagues leaving drinks were both sad and very enjoyable. It's hard to believe that he won't be here anymore....he seemed pleased to be going though. Your message was read out and he was clearly moved by your words...see, you are a star even when not present! WR

I do hope Wheely had a suitable send off! DJ

I have so much enjoyed reading your epic e-mails. Sounds like you are having a ball. Oh no poor Wheely! I'm going to be out in San Francisco in May. If you tell me where he is I can leave a card or flowers. Look forward to hearing more of your travels across the States and hope to see you before too long. EM

Yet more messages of bereavement; how thoughtful.

Day Eighty
Flight Seventeen, Toronto

Dropped off at Las Vegas Airport, the donkey train made its way to the Air Canada terminal to check in for our flight to Toronto. I instantly forgot we were still in Las Vegas as the airport terminal was so different from the one we had arrived at originally. There were no one-armed bandits to be found, and rather irritatingly, there was most definitely no smoking allowed anywhere. We enquired as to where the business class lounge was and with short shrift were told there wasn't one. Damn and blast, I wanted to get to work on my e-mail.

It proved to be a very long day and indeed the whole day was spent travelling. This was the price you had to pay to get to these magnificent destinations; a lot of time spent in airports, in my opinion, was a very small price to pay.

We arrived in Toronto late at night, so much so we didn't have enough time to see anything. A walk in downtown Toronto would have been good, but alas it was not to be. We made our way to our bedroom, noted it had a nice bed, and promptly got into it.

Day Eighty-one
Niagara Falls

First thing in the morning we went in search of a car rental outlet. The only reason for coming to Toronto was to go to Niagara Falls. Perhaps if we had allowed ourselves a little more time we could have visited many other destinations in Canada. Having gone from scorching temperatures, we arrived at Niagara Falls to find that it was now snowing. We had indeed encountered many climactic changes during our travels, and this was no exception. It was a filthy day.

The hotel that we booked was fantastic, and everything about the room was absolutely perfect; the bathroom was a very good disabled one and had all the bars in the right places, hooray Canada. We had slightly pushed the boat out on this one and selected a hotel right next to Niagara Falls that gave us a clear and full view. The view from our bedroom was to die for; only not today it wasn't, as the weather had closed in, limiting our view of this spectacular sight. As they say, tomorrow is another day.

We went out for a walk, and lo and behold we managed to stumble across yet another branch of Starbucks. It was so cold that I momentarily forgot the size of my increasing waist and suggested that we go to warm up and have a cappuccino and a muffin. On the way back to the hotel we found a shop selling gloves. David's hands were so cold they were practically blue. Usually his hands are

307

kept warm by gripping the handlebars, but not today.

Without warning, the drain staged a comeback. Was I tired or was I cold? I really didn't know. Suffice it to say it completely ruined the rest of my day and, of course, David's.

My mood had undergone a dramatic change; having been happy and carefree, the life had now been sucked out of me. My mobility had deteriorated so much so that I was incapable of doing anything, and I screamed with absolute frustration. I found myself crying in such a way that it frightened me, and when I did try to speak, it was completely inaudible. I was on my journey down the big black hole. I knew for a fact that today was another day I wished I was dead, I didn't want to live in this world anymore, I didn't want to live like this, and for David to do everything he had to do for me was just unbearable.

Day Eighty-two

Thankfully, a new day and a new disposition, life must go on, and I needed to dig down deep within myself; David deserves a lot more from me.

The sun was shining and we were informed that the weather conditions of yesterday had been apparently unseasonable to be like this. The falls looked even more magnificent with the sun shining on them. We were seeing yet another natural wonder of the world and heard the thunder of the falls crashing, felt the mist, and saw the wonder, which is Niagara Falls. A powerful passion stirred within me. It was utterly breathtaking, and I was consumed with love and lust.

This feeling reminded me of how I felt when we visited Brazil, more specifically the Iguazu Falls, when I was staggered by the sheer volume of water, magnitude, and beauty.

We viewed Niagara Falls from every angle possible and of course took many photographs, which would be interesting to compare with the ones we took yesterday; I felt the latter would no doubt be deleted. We really wanted to witness the view from another dimension so we found ourselves making tracks towards the Skylon Tower, Niagara's most famous landmark right next to the falls. Yet another view and of course an awful lot more photographs, just how many could one take? The answer

Nicky Dalladay

is loads.

Having seen the falls from every angle known to man we got in the car and headed back to Toronto to return the car to its rightful owners, Avis. Miles covered: two hundred and seventy.

We walked toward the CN Tower, which was advertised as Canada's wonder of the modern world. With the little time we had allowed ourselves to visit Toronto we felt it was necessary to go up the tower, which rather sounds as though somebody was forcing us, which was not accurate, we wanted to go there. The tower defines the Toronto skyline at a height of 1,815 feet, five inches, and the CN tower is Canada's National Tower. Tickets purchased and the lift located we were on our way up. The first level at 1,122 feet had an observation area that we were able to walk completely around, enabling us to take in the views, whilst inside was the famous glass floor. David wheeled me back and forth over the glass to ensure that I could see everything, and of course leave a few dirty tyre marks. I was sure somebody would thank us later for that one. We noticed just how small everything was; the people and the cars resembled dinky toys.

Unfortunately, because of wheelchair restrictions we were prohibited access from going into the pod, the highest point. But luckily for us, there was a really nice woman, a member of staff not just any old woman who took pity on us managed to sneak us up in a lift on our way down, which was very clever of her. She enabled us to get a view through a small round window near to the very top; she had gone above and beyond the call of duty.

My Travels with Wheely

This evening, we went to the Hard Rock Café for dinner. Yes, I had a burger and chips, what else should one have at the Hard Rock Café? One could easily deduce from this I was not on a diet and wasn't planning to go on one in the foreseeable future; I was on an extended holiday. Whilst I thought about it, it had become pretty obvious that I had no intention of quitting smoking. Anyway, there we were, enjoying munching on our burger and chips when suddenly all of the staff jumped on to the bar and began to entertain the assembled diners by singing and dancing. It was brilliant. What a wonderful way to finish our stay in Toronto.

Day Eighty-three
Flight Eighteen, Boston

At Toronto Airport check-in desk for our flight to Boston, we were confronted by what I could only describe as a very cold woman who was instantly named "Mrs. Frosty." I would have to get cracking with warming her up a little. So I did what comes naturally to me, I engaged in conversation with her, put a smile on her face, and hey presto, the transformation was complete.

Although I got a little bit more than I bargained for; she had warmed up so much she had become very tactile, which reminded me of those long-gone days in Vietnam. As so many people did, and still do, once they have established what is wrong with me they proceed to tell me that they know somebody who has got MS. Mrs. Frosty said that I was indeed a "gung-ho gal," something like that anyway, apparently I reminded her of a close friend of hers who also had multiple sclerosis, but she had died, and even I wasn't quite ready for that one. My job was done, I had cured Mrs. Frosty, and she was now very sweet and helpful. She was very encouraged and admired us both for getting on with our lives. This statement in itself was by no means unusual. We had met an awful lot of people on our travels who had expressed similar comments.

Toronto Airport seemed to be awash with paperwork. Everywhere we turned we were presented with another

My Travels with Wheely

form to complete, we didn't really mind, it was their country and their rules. I firmly believed we had at last reached the point of no return and certainly no more forms; after all, we were at the entrance of the airplane. But what was that in David's hands? A form. We had met many friendly and nice people en route to the airplane but the final one had to be one of the nicest men, he laughed and joked with us and said I was beautiful. He was probably lying, but I didn't really care, as far as I was concerned, he had said the right thing at the right time. Score for this airport was awarded, and because of him alone it was ten.

Up in the air once more, we had now left Toronto and were on our way to Boston, USA. At Boston Airport we had arranged to pick up a hire car. Perfect — there it was, ready and waiting for us, a white Pontiac. David works his magic again, the overlarge suitcase, the small suitcase we bought in Bangkok, the fold-up walking frame, the now shrunken computer case, me, and finally "Wheels," the second-hand wheelchair we had purchased in San Francisco, were all packed into the car. We were off, in search of our hotel. We had been issued with a very small map of the area which at first glance seemed okay, but later decided it was somewhat lacking in detail.

What should have been a relatively quick journey actually turned into a four-hour one. We were looking for 250 Franklyn Street but hadn't taken on board just how long this road was and the very peculiar numbering system. Anyway, to cut a long story short, we ended up at the opposite end of where we should be and were now in downtown Boston. I urged David to stop and ask one

Nicky Dalladay

of the natives where we were, in order to put us back on track. Why is it that men are so reticent about having to ask for directions? Male ego, methinks.

At last, we finally arrived at the Langham Hotel, Boston, Massachusetts; a celebratory cigarette was needed and of course had. We were both slightly taken aback; the hotel was just striking. The team on the reception desk were lovely and very accommodating. We were only going to be there for two nights but instantly decided that we would like Boston, so we headed off and felt sure that we would probably find a nice bar to have a drink in.

Day Eighty-four

A lovely day was spent in Boston. First we went to a coffee shop near to the hotel to get our bearings. We met a lovely man named Bill who was from Boston, his accent a strong Bostonian one, rich and warm, and he was a very hospitable man, a pleasure to have met him.

I don't know why but we found ourselves wandering in the direction of the New England Telephone Headquarters Building, and before we knew it, we were inside. We were standing in the lobby of the building and gazing in sheer wonderment at the site that beheld us. It was the most magnificent mural, portraying the story of the "Telephone Men and Women at Work." The mural forms a complete oval one hundred sixty feet long by twelve feet high. Its 197 life-size figures dramatically depict three groupings of telephone people at work. The work was completed in 1951 but sadly, I don't know how long it took to produce such a magnificent piece of art. There had been and are some amazingly talented people in the world.

In the afternoon we went on a trolley bus tour, the Green and Orange route around Boston, which gave us a flavour of the city. It was lovely and interesting but we were unable to take many pictures because you were too close to the buildings. The trolley bus driver was a fine old character who chortled and chuckled his way around the circuit and amused us no end. It seemed to be customary to ask everybody where they were from and it quite surprised

Nicky Dalladay

me as he was only asking which state in America they were from. He then turned his attention to us and asked if we were from outside America. I wondered what made him think that, when we said that we were British he said to the rest of the occupants on the bus, be nice to them they are our only allies; many a true word said in jest.

In the evening we went to an Italian restaurant just two hundred yards from the hotel, which the concierge had recommended and booked for us. The restaurant was called Umbria and the food was exquisite. It was so far removed from our previous Italian restaurant experience in San Francisco, and we doubted there would be any dodgy tummy incidents. During the course of dinner I was rather intrigued by three of the waiting staff who just stood doing nothing. I thought to myself how peculiar it was that people got paid for doing nothing; they could have at least pretended to be busy.

Day Eighty-five
Edgecombe, Maine

We left Boston to commence our drive around New England. Our first stop was going to be in Maine, and the drive there was quite spectacular and the glorious weather made everything look so beautiful. We had two nights reserved in a motel overlooking a bay which we found with relative ease, but I couldn't help but smirk when I saw the place as it really reminded me of Bates Motel from the film *Psycho*. Come to think of it, the person who opened the front door looked strangely familiar. The accommodation was quite comfortable and clean, although a little tired looking.

We went for a stroll but it appeared that New England was very quiet and could be described as closed. We found one shop and made a meal out of walking around it for as long as possible; it was an odd place that seemed to sell everything, but nothing you wanted. We also found an eating establishment that wasn't a restaurant and wasn't a café but was somewhere that you could buy food to take out. With our tummies rumbling and no clear sign of anywhere else to eat we made the most of what was available to us.

Back at Bates Motel, we sat on our veranda overlooking the bay and eating the food wc had purchased. I noticed that they had put out tomorrow's breakfast in our bedroom and thought to myself that was real forward planning.

Day Eighty-six

Both up bright and breezy but alas no shower to start the day with as the disabled facilities were nonexistent. Rather peculiarly I was quite pleased that we didn't have a shower as there was every chance that it would have a plastic shower curtain, which meant there would be the possibility of someone behind it wielding a knife; that's the problem with an overactive imagination.

We breakfasted on the veranda and laughed as we unwrapped the plastic packaging which concealed our food for the morning. I have chosen not to write about it for the very reason it doesn't deserve it. We decided to take off and have a drive around, the properties in this area were a typical New England weatherboard design, and they were all gorgeous. It was a very peaceful place and there were certainly not many people around.

We had had a beautiful day out but decided to head back toward the motel. Stupid us, we had actually forgotten there weren't any restaurants or cafes where we were staying, so once again we found ourselves visiting the eating establishment of the night before for another take out of something or other. We sat on the veranda again but I felt that there was something missing. What could it be? I wondered, perhaps it was a clay pipe and a rocking chair, for Ma and Pa to rock side by side watching the sun go down.

Day Eighty-seven
Lincoln, New Hampshire

Phew, we were safely away from Bates Motel, such a strange old place. We had a lovely drive and just enjoyed the beauty.

We arrived at our next destination. The hotel was a fairly modern build so you could say that our hopes and expectations had been raised somewhat; as a person, I am still an optimist. Our bedroom was on the ground floor, excellent. Number one box ticked. On to the second box, we tried to a get into the bedroom. It had a very heavy fire door and David had to wedge it open with our very large suitcase; I knew it would to come into its own eventually. Now in the room David goes to investigate the bathroom facilities, and as per usual, we had booked a disabled room, only to find that once again we were confronted with a small tub with a shower in it. Third box resulted in a big fat cross.

We went to the reception desk to inform them that the bathroom was not in the least bit disabled friendly. Imagine my horror when "Mrs. Bothered," who was incidentally sat on her derrière reading a magazine, appeared to have some sort of neck ailment preventing her from lifting her head to look at us, told us that their hotel was responsible for hosting a annual handicapped convention. What sort of response was that it was clearly irrelevant. I merely said that their guest room book in the bedroom invited me

Nicky Dalladay

to make a complaint if I felt the need should arise, the moment had presented itself, and I was just doing what I was invited to do. She simply turned her nose up, advised us there was nothing she could do and carried on reading her "Horse and Hounds" magazine, charming.

As we were only there for one night, I wasn't going to let Mrs. Bothered affect me. You think I would have learned by now that obtaining a disabled bathroom with a walk-in shower was never going to be easy. I had no idea it was going to be virtually impossible.

We smiled a sickly sweet smile to Mrs. Bothered on our way out to see what Lincoln had to offer. Something we were by no means expecting, we stumbled upon a skiing resort, which was quite amazing, and it had very wide pistes and was so unlike Austria, where in the past we had done the majority of our skiing. To be forewarned is to be forearmed, so it was a shame we didn't notice the lack of people around. Ah, we thought, it was around après ski time and assumed that everybody had made haste to the bar, so when in Rome and all that, we did exactly the same. Only there was nobody in the bar; it was completely deserted, I guessed that on this occasion, we would not be having a stein or two of beer.

Back in the car we had a drive around and it was a very pretty area. We found ourselves in the direction of Woodstock, not to be confused with the famous Woodstock in upstate New York. We stopped at a restaurant and tried the famous American meat loaf before wending our way back to Mrs. Bothered. If we were in luck, she would be off duty by now.

Day Eighty-eight
Stowe, Vermont

On the road again, or rather the State Highway, we had managed to get ourselves slightly lost, so we pulled over to consult the map. David did, anyway. I kept myself occupied by having a cigarette. Whilst David was having his consultation with himself we hadn't noticed the police car that pulled up behind us. I instantly thought we had done something wrong; perhaps it was illegal to smoke on the side of the road. Just showed how wrong you could be, the rather dashing young policeman had stopped to inquire if we were okay, as it was obvious from the car number plates that it was a rented car. We told him where we were looking for and he very kindly pointed us in the right direction.

We followed the directions and for all intents and purposes we looked as though we had arrived, but there was something wrong, the hotel looked out of this world and certainly not something we were expecting. But before David gets me out of the car he does his usual thing and checks out the bathroom, and again it was no good. No problem, said the man in his lederhosen, he would upgrade us at no extra cost to a suite, as it was a very quiet time of year.

He told us that we were in time for afternoon tea in the day lounge, so without delay we went to the lounge. I realized that once we had got in there his lederhosen

Nicky Dalladay

was not out of place. Well, they were really when you considered we weren't in Europe, but the women serving tea were wearing their dirndl dresses. We were staying in the Trapp Family Lodge, and this place was steeped in history of the Von Trapp family, who had fled from Austria in 1938, travelling around Europe, giving concert tours, and in 1939 the family settled in America. The baron died in 1947 whilst Maria lived until 1987. We walked around the family burial plots on the grounds. I didn't know who now owned this fine establishment we were in, but you could say they were making the very best of the history that was contained here, and you really couldn't blame them.

Suddenly it reminded me of a family of seven that we had seen in Hawaii that were all wearing matching red Hawaiian shirts. They would fit in quite well here.

Having had the benefit of fresh air and a walk outside we were now in a position where we were looking forward to having dinner, and what a wonderful meal it was. David yodelled his way whilst pushing me back to our suite.

Day Eighty-nine
Williamstown

Had we been blessed with the benefit of hindsight we would have certainly stayed in the Von Trapp Family Lodge for just one extra night, but we weren't, so once more the car was loaded up and we were on our way making tracks to our next destination. The scenery was very pretty and we passed some lovely buildings. We arrived at our hotel and were greeted by the owner, who welcomed us to Williamstown. He was an extremely polite gentleman and most emphatic in telling us that should we need anything during our visit we only had to ask.

We decided to go for a walk to see what Williamstown had to offer. There were fabulous buildings, and we learned that it was a college town. We found a nice café and sat outside enjoying the sunshine and admiring the buildings. All was going very well. That was, until I lit a cigarette. A man pounced on me from nowhere. I felt sure he was going to apprehend and arrest me. What on Earth had I done? He was glaring at me in the most unfriendly manner; did I not realize I was not allowed to smoke within a six metre radius of any college building? No, I can honestly say that I didn't, but I certainly did now. This smoking business was obviously going to be a little tricky here, as we were completely surrounded by college buildings.

Day Ninety

We ventured forth to see what else Williamstown had to offer; it was a glorious day and we were not in a hurry. We happened upon the Clark Museum and the cultural experience inside was enhanced by the great natural beauty of the Clark's one hundred forty-acre campus. The setting offered splendid views of the green mountains of Vermont. The museum welcomed visitors all year round to experience its outstanding collection of European and American art. Opened in 1955 by Singer sewing machine heir Robert Sterling Clark and his wife, Francine, the institute has built upon the couple's extraordinary art, sculpture, and silver and porcelain collection.

We sat outside and had a coffee and sandwich. I took a risk and lit up a cigarette; hooray, the six metre exclusion zone didn't apply here, how did I know that? Because clever old me spotted an ashtray.

As we strolled back toward the hotel we noticed countless fantastic buildings dating back to the seventeenth century, new and modern as far as we were concerned, but I guessed their history had to start somewhere; I chastised myself for feeling so British and being sniffy about our heritage.

Day Ninety-one
Rhode Island

The time had come to load the car once more as today we were continuing our journey toward to Rhode Island. Another day spent in the car ohing and arhing at the beautiful surroundings and of course scenery. Tonight we were staying in a Best Western Inn. We had no problem finding it and David was delighted to report that the bathroom had a walk-in shower. Hooray, I was beginning to feel a bit smelly.

We went into town and were over the moon to discover there was a wealth of restaurants and fine eating establishments for us to dither about choosing. We felt this choice hadn't been available to us for a long time, so we were careful to ensure we picked exactly the right restaurant, though in reality, we would not know how good it was until we ate there. So the restaurant had now been selected, and we entered with excitement. We needn't have worried. We had the most sumptuous feast: lobster filled with scallops and crab meat and a bottle of Veuve Clicquot; welcome back, decadence, my old friend.

Day Ninety-two
Cape Cod

Now having breakfast at the Best Western Inn I was pleased with myself that I had taken note of the egg options available when we were in San Francisco. Simple, it was over easy for me and sunny-side up for David, and I was now getting the hang of this.

After a good hearty breakfast we hit the road again to drive to Cape Code and arrived just in time for lunch and were told if we wanted to eat we would have to hurry as the restaurant would be closed for the next two days. So we hit the buffet as we realized the consequences of this meant we were faced with the prospect of not eating for the next two days, great.

Day Ninety-three

The hotel itself was outstandingly beautiful and certainly offered the best bedroom accommodation we had seen in New England. They actually got it! The word disabled and the words walk-in shower were actually possible. They could do it, and I very nearly cried for joy. It was amazing that coming across this room made you nearly forget just how awful some of the other places were.

We went for a stroll downtown to see what was about; sadly, very little, but fortunately I managed to console myself by purchasing a new top. At least I would look smart whilst eating thin air. We got in the car, drove along the coast and 'round to the peninsula, stopped and got out, and David was able to wheel me onto the sandy beach. It was a glorious feeling, the warmth of the sun and sand between my toes; I was a very happy girl.

Back at the hotel, tonight was our last night before we headed back to Boston tomorrow. David went to the hotel to see if the bar was open, but no, it was shut. Luckily for us we had a bottle of wine and some potato chips — "crisps" — how the mighty had fallen once again. Later on we went to the hotel reception and spoke to a lovely girl who was manning the fort in the absence of all her colleagues, who seemed to be away. We asked if it was possible to have a coffee, and at first she said no, but then said she was about to make one for herself and would make us one as well. I asked her if there was

Nicky Dalladay

a chance of a chocolate chip cookie and she said yes of course. David looked at me in such an odd way that I interpreted it to mean that if I were to eat any more cookies I would end up looking like one. Was he trying to tell me something?

Day Ninety-four
Boston

Today we drove back to Boston and dropped the Pontiac off. We had covered 1,277 miles on our drive around New England. In retrospect, New England hadn't really been the best choice, as most places we visited seemed to be closed, though at the right time of year I was almost certain it would have a lot more to offer.

Arrived at our hotel back in Boston, and it wasn't the same one we had stayed in when we first arrived, but nonetheless it looked very pleasant. We felt rather confident that the room would be perfect. Oops, what was I thinking? Just because the last one had been good I had incorrectly assumed that this would be fine as well, silly me. We were shown to our room and this time the hotel industry really did surpass themselves. We had to change rooms three times until finally we were in a room that was perfect.

We dumped our bags to go and hit the shops. I saw my final Starbucks of the trip, so naturally we went in. We were quietly having our coffee, when all of a sudden David leapt from his seat and ran outside. My god what had happened? Had he seen someone being mugged or even worse, somebody killed? I didn't know what to think, and I was worried. Before I knew it he arrived back with a grin on his face. He had seen somebody leaving Starbucks carrying a Banana Republic bag and wanted to know where the shop

Nicky Dalladay

was. I spurted my coffee out and roared with laughter. What a fine time to decide to get in touch with your feminine side and want to go shopping. Why on Earth not? He has surely earned a reward or two for such devotion to duty. We located Banana Republic and he had a massive spending spree. I did say at the outset I was going to get him back. We had just passed Tiffany and Co., so we turned around and went in.

With the amount of shopping we had just done, combined with the things we had accumulated on our journey, we realized it was necessary to purchase another bag just to enable us to pack everything up before getting our flight to go home.

E-mail Received

I guess by now that you're on your last leg of your trip. I'm really looking forward to seeing you on your return to the UK. I'm having leaving drinks on the twenty-eighth at the Broadgate Circle. DJ

Fantastic, we haven't even arrived home yet and already had several invitations to go out.

Day Ninety-five
Flight Nineteen

The hotel room resembled a refugee camp. Items were strewn all across the floor, and some serious packing was about to take place. I just let David get on with it since he knew what he was doing; as I sat and watched him do this I was consumed with nothing but love and admiration.

Now at the airport for our penultimate flight Boston to Washington DC. The donkey train made its final journey before being dismantled and stowed in various parts of the plane. I have just enough time to send my final message home.

Ninth E-mail
Time to go home

Somewhat hurried as I am running out of time and dollar bills but want to send it before we get home.

San Francisco was great but too short, with having to find a replacement for Wheely, which as you will imagine was not easy. In our search for a suitable alternative we had a hell of a taxi ride through the streets of San Francisco. Wow, it reminded me of those bygone days of watching *The Streets of San Francisco* and *Bullet*. We did manage to buy another wheelchair and it will take a while to run in.

Nicky Dalladay

On the way back we found it hard to find a taxi big enough to take two wheelchairs so set about walking back to the hotel. En route there was a couple of San Francisco cops who stopped us to enquire where we were going and kindly informed us we had a "hell of a way to go." We explained that we couldn't find a big enough cab. Before we knew it one of the cops was in the middle of the road pulling over the first cab he saw and telling the cab driver he could fit the two wheelchairs in, and then whilst one was helping David with the brace of wheelchairs the other was shoving me in the back of the cab, and I really do mean shoving, but my legs had gone on a "stiffy" and wouldn't bend, so he just kept on shoving, and hey presto, there I was lying across the back seat. Who said the age of chivalry was dead?

The same day as losing Wheely we managed to see off our second camera we bought on our last day in Oz. So, one new set of wheels and our third camera and we set off for Las Vegas, hoping to retrieve the additional expenditure by playing the tables and in the belief that nothing can possibly go wrong.

We arrived in Vegas, and my goodness what a very big, loud, and busy place this is, in the middle of the desert. You'd have thought it was nice and secluded. Our hotel for the night was the Luxor, which had a pyramid and a sphinx the size of Loughton, no kidding, it was very big. We walked up and down the Strip and checked out a few of the hotels, some of which were better than others, the most impressive was probably the Paris Hotel boasting a replica of the Eiffel Tower.

My Travels with Wheely

We did have a little flutter, and I do mean little, bearing in mind neither of us are gamblers (with money), and we parted with $1.50. You will not be surprised to hear we didn't win a cent, I wonder why?

We left Vegas for our trip to the Grand Canyon and were supposed to be picked up at 05.00 but this was changed to 13.00. This was the start of real U.S. inefficiency at its best. (Profound apologies to all of our USA friends.) We arrived at the GC early evening and were taken to this lodge in the National Park; well, David went to check out the bathroom, which he's had to do since day one, and yes, another bath — or I should say "tub"!

The next morning we were due to see the sunrise. Can you imagine how beautiful that would be, illuminating the GC? Well, we were up bright eyed and bushy tailed at 04.30 to be picked up at 05.10, but we waited and waited and at 05.30 the pickup arrived. The long and the short of this is we missed it. We were freezing cold and poor David developed frostbite. Well, nearly.

Fly back to Vegas for a one night stay in the Bellagio Hotel. What a gorgeous hotel, such magnificent fountains and displays, a true delight.

Where next? A quick trip to Canada, Toronto, as we hear there's a bit of a waterfall to see nearby. This was a bit of whirlwind tour but most definitely worth it. Where on Earth does all that water keep coming from with such force? Again, it was another joy to behold. Back to Toronto, up the CN tower, and down and off for our next destination, Boston.

Nicky Dalladay

With heavy heart we realize we now start the last leg of this epic journey around the World. What a lovely place to end, on a Boston and New England driving tour. This time in our Pontiac, no open top this time, its freezing but the skies are blue and the sun is shining.

We head for Maine. Wow wee, what a beautiful place, or more specifically Boothbay Harbor (note I have slipped in to U.S. spelling). Must say we rather think New England is shut, as this is definitely out of season, but one might say perfect, since there are no tourists. On to Lincoln, New Hampshire, weather still on side and we are at the bottom of a ski slope; the lifts have just stopped and we are looking for a beer, not a chance, there is not one single person, we watched the last three come down the slopes and … go.

On to Stowe, Vermont, and oh dear me, my fantasy has finally become a reality, yes we are staying in the Von Trapp Family Lodge, eek, how fantastic is that? Sadly we wouldn't be there for the Sound of Music evening, drat and double drat. You'd think you were in Austria right now.

Well, we've had a lot of fun and enjoyed each other's company for the last three months. There have been many tears but even more laughter on our journey around the World, but we wouldn't change this experience for anything, and if there are any regrets it's only that we didn't make it six months. The World is a very big place and we just didn't have enough time in some of the places like NZ.

My Travels with Wheely

When we embarked on this journey I was blissfully ignorant of the demands this epic would put on David, but you will not be surprised to hear he dealt with every situation brilliantly and always with a smile, what a "top bloke" he truly is.

We thank all of those who sent us e-mails; they were both informative and amusing and much appreciated. Thanks for your thoughts and kind words about "Wheely"; we did indeed give him the send off he deserved!

When we arrive home we look forward to seeing you.

Love to everyone
The DallAwayDays
xxxx

Nicky Dalladay

Flight Twenty
Washington DC to London, Heathrow

The airplane was boarded for the final time. Our journeys have entailed several modes of transport to cover approximately thirty thousand miles.

We have had a fabulous time. It didn't go quickly and in fact you might even say it went slowly; I wished it had been longer but of course that was easy to say after the event. What did we get wrong? We could have been more organized on the luggage front and thought more about the amount of time spent at each destination. In some places we clearly hadn't allowed sufficient time. It was only now when we were on the verge of going home that we realized just how tired we both were. We had rushed around and not given ourselves adequate time to relax. We thought we had planned for this, but clearly we got it slightly wrong.

We were fortunate to have met some tremendous people on our travels that we are unlikely to see ever again, and we had many amazing experiences; my health can deteriorate, but nobody can take my memories or feelings away from me.

We arrived back in the United Kingdom on a beautiful spring day and went into our home. Suddenly we felt lost and alone. It was all over and we had actually done and it neither of us could believe it.

Our closest friends had rallied around, flicked a duster here and there, and ensured that there were provisions in our fridge, and a welcome home card with a bunch of flowers. I'm not sure why, but I started crying, I was full of

My Travels with Wheely

E-mails Received

Welcome back to blighty! Oh my God, what a fantastic trip, can't believe you are now back. Your e-mails have been the highlight and only reason to come into work, nothing disturbs me whilst reading them, and I start the day with a smile. Well done, you have achieved so much, poor old Wheely, faithful to the end! Look forward to seeing you again soon. TJ

Home now…so how are you feeling? I would guess that you are not back to "normal" just yet, but then, what is normal? Very mixed feelings? We want to take David, and you too Nicky? to see the other B-52. GD

That was certainly quite an adventure. The ferry trip from Wellington was particularly scary just reading about it. Our time in New Zealand and Australia was fun and did not provide much that was frightening except the gain in weight as we polished off all those delicious bottles of wine. We really enjoyed meeting you at the Sounds of Silence Dinner and then reading about your exploits along the way. M&L

Welcome home and thank you for having included me on your trip newsletter. You appear to have had a brilliant time. I expect you are busy at the moment planning your next trip to some other exotic place, although I expect that Loughton has its attractions for a month or two whilst you rest up. RH

I have been following your trip with complete admiration

Nicky Dalladay

and yes a certain amount (a lot) of jealousy as we have only ever got as far as Cyprus. I've been watching too, and dropping in the names of the places you have been into Google images as I read your messages it has provided a real flavour of where you are. So trying to picture how you have got up down, around, in and out of some of the difficult places I cannot imagine but hey, I know you Nicky and if it's a challenge it makes you try harder. Poor Wheely. SS

We were both exhausted and had demanded so much from our bodies. It was only now that the realization started to sink slowly in about what we had actually accomplished. Whilst not everything was perfect, it was never going to be, but there were an awful lot of things that were. We travelled to destinations we had only dreamt of before, we had actually done it we had now fulfilled our dream and were immensely proud of ourselves.

AFTERWORD

It is now nearing the end of 2010 and by completing my book I have just relived our whole journey, and for that I am grateful. This process has been a hugely cathartic experience, more so than seeing a shrink. In all honesty, now, four years later, we would not be able to undertake a journey of such magnitude; as I said at the beginning you can't take anything in life for granted.

True to form, my condition has deteriorated and I continue to grieve when yet another part of my body ceases to function; it is the only way I can deal with it. Fortunately, the alien is an infrequent visitor but the drain likes to remind me of its existence far too regularly for my liking. None of us know what the future holds but one thing I do know, life is for living!

As I found inner peace by the sea in Australia and the lakes in New Zealand, we make the time to ensure that we go to the seaside to recapture that feeling at home.

David has slipped quite nicely into his role of looking after the house, caring for me, and of course taking pride in doing his washing. Whilst the mundane things are necessary, more importantly he deserves a break from me and was lucky enough to discover and pursue his love of learning about art.

I have spent time struggling to find something I really enjoy doing, which trust me has not been easy. A couple

Nicky Dalladay

of years ago I took up horse riding for the disabled and am glad that I experienced that when I could, as I have now had to give it up.

On the positive side, at last I have succeeded in finding something that I can truly enjoy. Of course I would adore to be dancing, but that is never going to happen. Earlier this year I joined a singing group and have already performed in two shows with them. When I was back on stage, I felt as though a small part of me had returned, the old me, and I love that feeling.

"It's a little bit funny, this feeling inside, I'm not one of those who can easily hide, I know it's not much, but it's the best I can do. My gift is my song and this one's for you. I hope you don't mind that I put down in words, how wonderful life is while you're in the world."

Extracts from "Your Song"
Elton John and Bernie Taupin

Lightning Source UK Ltd.
Milton Keynes UK
172593UK00001B/1/P